CW00949981

BLITZ
HOSPITAL

BLITZ HOSPITAL

TRUE STORIES OF NURSING IN WARTIME LONDON

PENNY STARNS

Dedicated to my Grandmother Florence Reid,
a survivor of the London Blitz.

First published 2018

The History Press
The Mill, Brimscombe Port
Stroud, Gloucestershire, GL5 2QG
www.thehistorypress.co.uk

© Penny Starns, 2018

The right of Penny Starns to be identified as the Author
of this work has been asserted in accordance with the
Copyright, Designs and Patents Act 1988.

All rights reserved. No part of this book may be reprinted
or reproduced or utilised in any form or by any electronic,
mechanical or other means, now known or hereafter invented,
including photocopying and recording, or in any information
storage or retrieval system, without the permission in writing
from the Publishers.

British Library Cataloguing in Publication Data.
A catalogue record for this book is available from the British Library.

ISBN 978 0 7509 8249 8

Typesetting and origination by The History Press
Printed and bound in Great Britain by TJ International Ltd

CONTENTS

ACKNOWLEDGEMENTS

The process of writing this book has been greatly assisted by the military and civilian nurses who generously recounted their wartime experiences for my research. They include: Monica Baly, Mary Bates, Glenys Branson, Constance Collingwood, Gertrude Cooper, Ursula Dowling, Brenda Fuller, Anne Gallimore, Monica Goulding, Daphne Ingram, Anita Kelly, Margaret Kneebone, Sylvia Mayo, Kay McCormack, Anne Moat, Phyllis Thoms and Dame Margot Turner. The remarkable story of the latter is the subject of a separate book entitled *Surviving Tenko*. Dame Margot's oral history testimony is held in the Imperial War Museum Sound Archive. The families of Rose Evans, Gladys Tyler, Florence Johnson and Grace Davis have also provided me with valuable source material.

Special thanks are due to the late Dr Monica Baly for her kindness, wisdom and guidance in the field of nursing history. Monica remained a very dear friend until her death in 1998. Thanks are also due to my PhD mentor Professor Rodney Lowe for his expertise in the field of welfare history. I am indebted to Captain Jane Titley, ARRC Matron-in-Chief of Queen Alexandra's Royal Naval Nursing Service 1991–94, and Colonel Eric Ernest Gruber Von Arni ARRC of the Queen Alexandra's Royal Army Nursing Service, for giving me valuable insights into the history and development of military nursing during the early stages of my research.

Archivists across the country have also assisted my research, especially those who are based at the Imperial War Museum, The National Archives, Royal London Hospital Archives, London Metropolitan Archives and the Royal College of Nursing Archives.

I thank my father Edward Starns for his consistent encouragement, and his vivid recollections of living through the Blitz. I am also grateful to those who have patiently listened to my ideas; these include Nigel Line, Michael and Rocha Brown, James and Lewis Brown, Joanna Denman, Catherine Nile and Margaret Taplin.

INTRODUCTION

In every war in our history, Britain has looked to the women to care
for the sick and wounded. It is women's work. The nurses never let us
down. Florence Nightingale lit a candle in the Crimea 85 years ago.
The women of today have kept it burning brightly, not only in France,
Egypt and Greece but in Poplar, Portsmouth, Liverpool, Hull and all
the other battlefields on the Home Front.

Government recruitment poster
Imperial War Museum 536/172/K9540

As a Ministry of Health nurse recruitment poster acknowledged, what
could be termed as being the 'front line' during the Second World
War was arbitrary. Medical staff were just as likely to be killed on the
Home Front as they were when working within international theatres
of war. Indeed, at the height of the Blitz, between September 1940 and
May 1941, Home Front medical staff were far more likely to be killed
or injured whilst administering emergency medical care than their
international counterparts. As the German Luftwaffe subjected Britain's
major cities and ports to unremitting waves of aerial bombardment,

doctors, nurses, first aiders, ambulance drivers and Air Raid Precaution workers constantly risked their lives to give urgent treatment to the severely wounded. Over 87,000 casualties were sustained during this period and city hospitals, especially in London, were working under extreme conditions. They were also experiencing acute staffing problems. A shortage of male doctors forced medical schools to open their doors to women, and nurses also extended their field of influence. A delighted senior nurse triumphantly wrote in the *Nurses' League Review* of The London Hospital:

> On March 1st the theatres were taken over by me and are now entirely run by the nursing staff. (Applause) This, as you will realise has meant a lot of reorganisation and it will take some time before they are running as we would wish. This, however, will mean that far more nurses can have theatre experience than was possible in the past.[1]

But as nurses' responsibilities increased, so did their workloads, and throughout the Blitz they worked at a furious pace. The diaries of London nurses reveal that they were confronted by a vast array of appalling injuries on a daily and nightly basis, 'charred bodies burnt black beyond recognition, gashed limbs and fractured spines. Gaping head injuries and bodies ripped apart by the force of bomb blasts.' London skies were frequently aglow with burning buildings, as a nurse recorded on 7 September 1940: 'One early evening I noticed that the city skyline was a brilliant red – it was just like a glorious sunset. Then I realised that if it was the sun, it was going down in the wrong place, because the glow was in the East.'[2]

Undoubtedly, the East End of London bore the brunt of the Blitz, which killed over 20,000 civilians in London alone. Survivors were cared for by staff at the city's hospitals, most of whom were an integral part of the government's official Emergency Hospital Scheme. Although source material is included from a variety of London hospitals, this book primarily follows the fortunes of two major London hospitals as they struggled to cope with mounting wartime casualties: St Thomas'

Hospital and The London Hospital (The Royal London from 1990 onwards). The diaries, letters and reports of medical and nursing staff highlight the many human stories of tremendous courage and hope that lived and breathed within the corridors, theatres and wards of London's hospitals during the Blitz.

Background History of British Hospitals

By the early twentieth century, most British hospitals fell into two categories, depending on their funding arrangements. First were the voluntary hospitals, which were maintained by charitable donations; second, the local authority hospitals, which were funded by regional authorities. Voluntary hospitals tended to be prestigious institutions where medical men carved out their reputations and careers. On the other hand, local authority hospitals tended to be more lowly establishments, often feared by members of the public because of their long-standing associations with nineteenth-century workhouses. St Thomas' and The London were both voluntary hospitals.

St Thomas' Hospital
St Thomas' Hospital was originally the infirmary of an Augustinian Priory dedicated to St Mary the Virgin. In 1173 it was afforded the name of St Thomas the Martyr, but the institution was destroyed by fire thirty-nine years later. Recognising that the infirmary had been a vital source of care for the sick, the Bishop of Winchester re-endowed the infirmary as an independent hospital, which was erected near London Bridge. However, like many other religiously affiliated establishments, St Thomas' was forcibly closed during the Reformation. It was not until the reign of King Edward VI that all monies and land were returned to St Thomas' and the hospital underwent a period of expansion. By the late seventeenth century, it was possible to discern a fledgling medical school, with both surgeons and physicians accepting apprentices and pupils for tuition.

During the eighteenth century, highly influential anatomists such as William Cheseldon gave lectures to medical students at St Thomas' and the hospital gained an excellent reputation for the study of anatomy and physiology, and clinical practice. For a time hospital governors controlled the medical school, but by 1860 control was handed back to physicians and surgeons. In the same year, Florence Nightingale established her first civilian training school for nurses at St Thomas', further enhancing the hospital's already prestigious reputation. As St Thomas' fame grew, further expansion was needed, and in 1868 Queen Victoria laid a foundation stone for an additional building, which was constructed near Westminster Bridge at Lambeth. Opened in 1871, this new building gave St Thomas' an extra 588 beds, and its prestige continued to grow.

During the First World War, 200 beds were set aside for military use and hospital staff played an important role in caring for the sick and injured. Crucially, new medical and surgical innovations had been implemented on the Western Front in response to modern warfare. These innovations, along with new medical research programmes, had significant implications for both military and civilian patients. Moreover, it was up to medical schools across Great Britain to ensure that this new-found knowledge was rapidly disseminated amongst all cohorts of medical students. Not content with merely passing on this new medical information, medical staff at St Thomas' were quick to initiate their own interwar research programmes. Thus, on the eve of the Second World War, St Thomas' was one of the most important teaching hospitals in London.[3]

The London Hospital

The London also began life as an infirmary, in 1740. Situated near the East End docks, it was dedicated primarily to healing the sick of merchant seamen and their families. Hospital buildings were initially located in Featherstone Street and Prescot Street, then in 1752 further building work began on Whitechapel Road. Referred to by staff as 'the front block', the Whitechapel building was opened in 1759. Further extensions were constructed to the east and west of the main building in 1770. By this stage, surgeons and physicians were actively encouraging pupils to accompany them on their ward rounds, and in 1785 the first lecture theatre opened its doors. Subsequently, The London Hospital Medical College was established, and from 1854 onwards came under the jurisdiction of the Hospital House Committee. Spurred on by the Industrial Revolution and a rapid growth in population, the demand for medical care increased. The London expanded accordingly, and by the turn of the century boasted over 1,000 beds. The London was the biggest voluntary, general hospital in Great Britain.

In addition to a medical college, The London also boasted an excellent nurse training programme. Matron Eva Luckes, who was a good friend of Florence Nightingale, had established a nurse training system similar to that at St Thomas' Hospital. However, some of Luckes' views on nurse training differed from those of her friend. Whilst Nightingale believed that nurse training should be entirely ward-based, Luckes argued that nurses needed a preliminary training school, to enable nurses to learn subjects such as anatomy and physiology. Emerging nurse reformers such as Ethel Bedford-Fenwick and members of the British Nursing Association (BNA) went a stage further, arguing that nurses needed state registration in order to provide protection for the sick. Suffragist Bedford-Fenwick also claimed that 'the nurse question is the woman question'. Subsequently, the drive for nurse registration was inextricably linked to the drive for female suffrage.

Eva Luckes, who was one of the youngest matrons in the country, introduced a series of educational reforms at The London but did not support the registration movement. Like Nightingale, she believed that nursing was a vocation that could not be tested by rigorous examinations. As Dr Baly has noted, Nightingale 'saw the registrationists as wanting to lower the standard, whereas they saw themselves as wanting to raise it and make nursing more exclusive'. Furthermore, she feared that nursing would be divided against itself, stating, 'I have terror lest the B.N.A.'s and the anti-B.N.A.'s should form hostile camps.'[4] Nightingale's fears were well founded, and nursing factions did indeed become politically fragmented. Yet despite her own reservations on the subject of registration, Luckes was convinced of the need to improve nurse education, and established one the first preliminary training schools for nurses in Britain.

Between 1914 and 1918, like all major hospitals, The London admitted its fair share of wounded soldiers, usually in groups of 300 or more. Often the injured were Belgian or French, which created considerable communication problems. Throughout this time, new techniques were introduced for dressing wounds, along with new nursing practices. In response to a growing need for nurse education, Eva Luckes compiled a series of detailed lectures for nurses, which were widely published. Further publications included guidance for nursing sisters. Luckes remained at The London until her death in 1919. During the interwar years, both the nursing school and medical college continued to thrive and grow in stature.

British Nursing

By 1939, British nursing was no longer a fledgling profession. Following a complex and often acrimonious thirty-year battle, the Nurse Registration Act was passed in 1919. This legislation gave nurses their long sought-after professional status, and offered some protection for the sick. Registration was achieved after a period of three years of hospital training and the passing of final examinations. Training schools were supervised by a General Nursing Council (GNC) but there was no uniform standard of training. Nurses worked long hours for poor pay, and were subjected to severe discipline and a myriad of petty rules. Consequently, wastage rates amongst probationer nurses were very high, with most hospitals losing over 50 per cent of their trainees within the first two years. Nurse training schools also had competition from other quarters. Whereas in the mid-nineteenth century young women were not particularly well educated, by 1900 their educational opportunities had increased. The 1870 Education Act had allowed school boards to widen their appeal to include more girls, and in 1869 Cambridge

University founded Girton, the first of its female colleges. Educational reforms increased women's career choices. There were 172,000 female schoolteachers in 1901 and 51,000 female civil servants by 1911.[5] Women's work also expanded during the First World War.

Thus, by the 1930s, British nursing faced a professional dilemma, which was never adequately addressed. Educated recruits did not make for a biddable workforce, and they needed something in the way of intellectual stimulus. But trying to marry the practical demands of nursing with intellectual endeavour was virtually impossible. Moreover, nurses were their own worst enemies, since 'the greatest obstacle to change came from nurses themselves. Nightingale nurses were reared in an atmosphere of obedience and conformity and second and third generations clung tenaciously to the principles that had raised them, first to respectability then to admiration. Obedience is inimical to innovation.'[6]

Incentives to enter the nursing profession were few and far between, and published advice for new probationers did nothing to encourage young girls into the profession, claiming that, as a result of spending their lives amid sorrow, suffering and the results of sin, nurses naturally became excessively morbid, introspective and depressed. According to nursing manuals, an antidote to this seemingly unavoidable descent into melancholia was for probationers to exercise rigorously in off-duty hours. Guidelines for new recruits also recommended regular church attendance, and trips to theatre or cinema productions to lift their minds out of the doldrums. However, probationers were often expected to forego their off-duty time because of staff shortages. Since they were also expected to attend lectures in their off-duty hours, there was precious little time for probationers to indulge in leisure activities, uplifting or otherwise.

Disincentives to nurse recruitment were identified in various official reports, and a government committee chaired by the Earl of Athlone published an interim report on the subject in 1939. The report concluded that in order to improve recruitment levels, it was necessary for the government to afford official recognition to assistant nurses and to subsidise voluntary hospitals, to enable these institutions to standardise training and improve salaries.[7] Not surprisingly, these recommendations were rejected by both government and nursing camps. Government officials were opposed to the idea of funding voluntary hospitals on economic grounds, whereas registered nurses vehemently objected to the proposed recognition of assistant nurses, believing this would undermine their hard-won status. With the outbreak of war in 1939, however, it soon became abundantly clear that both government and nursing camps would be forced to make concessions.

Sources

This book is based on primary source material obtained from an extensive collection of oral history testimonies and a wide variety of archives. These include the archives of St Thomas' Hospital, now located at the London Metropolitan Archives, and those of The Royal London. In addition, material has also been obtained from the British National Archives. This includes records of the General Nursing Council, the Ministry of Health, the Ministry of Labour and War Office files. Further material has been gleaned from the British Newspaper Library, the Imperial War Museum and the Royal College of Nursing Archives. Hansard House of Commons and House of Lords debates for the period were also examined in depth. Contemporary journals and newspapers were consulted at length. Of these, the *British Journal of Nursing* proved to be the most useful. It was not by any means the only nursing journal of the period, but it was the only one that remained constantly attuned, both to the global wartime political situation and to the more mundane problems faced by nurses themselves. Whilst *Nursing Illustrated* and other nursing periodicals relayed to their readers the virtues of beauty treatments, or introduced them to new wartime recipes, the *British Journal of Nursing* kept its readership up to date with current affairs and medical developments. As such, the paper appeared to represent the views of nurses who were politically aware and professionally motivated.

Additional material includes the author's published PhD thesis: *March of the Matrons* (2000), and the oral history testimonies of military and civilian nurses who worked during the Second World War; these were conducted by the author between 1993 and 1997. The BBC Radio 4 programme *Frontline Females* was based on the author's research and extracts are quoted in the text.

Notes

1 Nurse Littleboy, *The Royal London Hospital Nurses' League Review*, no. xi (1942), p. 8.
2 Recollections of Dame Kathleen Raven, *Royal College of Nursing, History of Nursing Journal*, vol. 3, no. 3 (1990), pp. 44–45.
3 For further information on St Thomas' role in the First World War please see London County Council Public Health ref: P.H./SHS/2.
4 Baly, M., *Florence Nightingale and the Nursing Legacy* (1997), p. 193.
5 *Report of the Census of England and Wales* (London: HMSO, 1911).
6 Baly, *op. cit.*, p. 219.
7 Early reports include *The Lancet Commission on Nursing 1932* and *The Interdepartmental Committee on the Nursing Service 1937*. The Athlone Committee was disbanded during the war but its findings were resurrected by the Rushcliffe Committee in 1943.

1

GETTING READY
FOR WAR

Despite the economic constraints of the interwar period, British
Government ministers began to prepare for the Second World War
as early as 1922. Civil defence strategies were discussed and medical
plans formulated. Moreover, even at this early stage of planning, it was
acknowledged that the main threat to civilians would come from the
air. This was confirmed by subsequent events in Europe. During the
Spanish Civil War, which began in 1936, Barcelona was subjected to over
340 air raids, which killed and maimed thousands of civilians. Thus, by
1937, British medical plans were based on the worst case scenario. As the
nation's capital city and centre of government, London was obviously
a major target for enemy action. The Imperial Defence Committee
estimated that during the first two years of war, between 1 and 2 million
hospital beds would be needed. They stockpiled thousands of cardboard
coffins and concluded that as soon as war was declared, at least 3,500 tons
of explosives would be dropped on London during the first twenty-four
hours, and 700 tons each day for at least a fortnight thereafter.[1]

Working on these alarming predictions, the government introduced
a number of civil defence measures and emergency medical schemes.
Blackout conditions were imposed, gas masks issued to adults and

children, Air Raid Precaution wardens and firefighters recruited and barrage balloons erected. Plans were unveiled to evacuate children and vulnerable adults away from major cities into the surrounding countryside, and staff at voluntary hospitals were conscripted and subjected to the jurisdiction of the Ministry of Health.[2] An Emergency Hospital Scheme was established, which divided the country into sectors with a matron and administrative staff for each sector, and this was supported by a system of first aid posts.

On 3 September 1939, Prime Minister Neville Chamberlain announced that Britain was at war with Germany. Almost immediately the Minister of Health, Walter Elliot, asked all hospitals across England to discharge as many patients as possible, in order to free up beds in readiness for air raid casualties. Patients in London hospitals who still needed care were evacuated by modified Green Line buses and ambulance trains to hospitals situated on the outskirts of the city. Many of London's voluntary hospitals became casualty clearing stations and outpatient departments closed virtually overnight.

On paper, medical preparations for war seemed to be more than adequate. However, there were not enough trained doctors and nurses to staff first aid posts, and a shortage of orthopaedic surgeons undermined the effectiveness of casualty clearing stations. Furthermore, medical experience gained during the Spanish Civil War had shown that unless casualties received immediate on-the-spot skilled attention, subsequent treatment was often useless. Senior Spanish orthopaedic surgeon Professor Trueta thus advised British medical personnel that highly skilled surgical teams needed to be at the centre of all major cities. He also advocated the implementation of his own signature five-step surgical treatment, which had saved many lives during the Spanish conflict. This included: immediate wound cleaning (within six hours of injury), excision of dead tissue, surgical treatment of fractures, wound drainage and closed immobilisation of fractures with plaster of Paris.

However, medical plans for British civilian casualties ran contrary to Professor Trueta's advice. Under the British Emergency Scheme, casualties were to receive basic care at first aid posts and hospitals designated as casualty clearing stations, and nearly all experienced surgeons would be waiting for casualties in centres remote from London. In view of Trueta's recommendations, senior doctors urged the Ministry of Health to revise existing arrangements.[3] They also questioned the role of voluntary hospitals within emergency schemes. The Chairman of the Formation Committee of the Air Raid Defence League, Sir Ralph Wedgwood, was also concerned, pointing out that:

> From almost every aspect, London hospitals are unsuitable to be casualty clearing stations. To make them bomb proof would be expensive and in most cases impossible. Far too many of our hospitals are liable to attack during an air raid. St Thomas's and Westminster are close to Battersea power station, which will be a target. Others are fatally close to the Thames. [4]

Yet despite these valid criticisms of emergency medical planning, the Ministry of Health remained intransigent. In the meantime, whilst doctors debated the merits and drawbacks of casualty clearance, registered nurses vented their own objections to medical policies emanating from Whitehall. These were primarily based on the need to protect their hard-won registered status, which in turn protected their patients from charlatans. Much to the dismay of registered nurses, Ministry of Health officials had substituted the word 'registered' with the word 'trained', which had no significance in law. The *British Journal of Nursing*, edited by Ethel Bedford-Fenwick, a leading protagonist of the nurse registration movement, was quick to defend professional status. In an article entitled 'The Duty and Privilege of the Registered Nurse in War', she praised registered nurses:

> Hand in hand with skilled medicine and surgery the ministrations of the registered nurse is the greatest remedial asset in war. No body of women hold more honourable status in the body politic than the members of our Naval Military and Air Force Nursing Services. In times of peace, wherever worn, their uniform commands respect, and

in times of war the devotion of our fighting forces is their inspiration and reward. The splendid body of registered nurses, now available in their tens of thousands for national service, will, we have no doubt, offer their skill and comfort to our sick and wounded, and although the reactionary Ministry of Health has ignored their legal title in every memorandum concerning the nursing service issued to the profession and the public, that lack of consideration will in no way affect their devotion to their King and country. As citizens of the British Empire Registered Nurses are all out to serve with the utmost ardour and devotion.[5]

Bedford-Fenwick was also quick to condemn the General Nursing Council (GNC) for their wholehearted support of a controversial government plan which, in a bid to ease nursing shortages, gave state recognition to a roll of assistant nurses. Not surprisingly, registered nurses, who were required to undertake three years' training and pass rigorous examinations, were up in arms at this decision. This situation was further compounded by the government's introduction of a Civil Nursing Reserve (CNR). Designed to supplement the civilian nursing services, the CNR contained mainly assistant nurses and auxiliaries, and from the outset caused considerable chaos. Hospital administrators, for instance, seizing an opportunity to reduce wage bills, were quick to use wartime conditions to replace registered nurses with CNR assistant nurses. Thus, within a mere two months, over 2,000 registered nurses in London had been made redundant. Registered nurses who had entered the armed forces were also frequently replaced by assistants. These problems were compounded by salary discrepancies. Registered nurses working for the CNR were paid the sum of £90 a year, whereas most registered nurses working in hospitals were paid £70 a year. Not surprisingly, many hospital nurses abandoned their positions and flocked to join the reserve.

Voluntary Aid Detachment nurses (VADs), recruited by the Order of St John of Jerusalem and the British Red Cross, were better organised than the CNR, and in most instances better trained. They supplemented both military and civilian medical services and in theory their training consisted of twelve first aid lectures, and between fifty and ninety hours of practical hospital experience. However, the government's central emergency committee was so desperate to recruit nurses for civilian first aid posts that VADs were assigned to duties even if they lacked the 'compulsory' fifty to ninety hours practical hospital training.[6]

With such an urgent emphasis on quantity rather than quality, and a sweeping dilution of the nursing profession with untrained personnel, Ministry of Health officials displayed an alarming degree of ignorance with regard to different levels of nursing expertise. For instance, at this stage, there were no government attempts to restrict the tidal wave of registered nurses who were rushing to join the armed forces, and seemingly no understanding of how this same tidal wave would seriously undermine civilian nursing services. Initially there were 30,000 women in the CNR, but only 7,000 of these were registered nurses. Moreover, despite the fact that civilian nursing services were severely understaffed, the CNR was restricted to working within the emergency services. The policy of emptying as many hospitals as possible in readiness for casualties had also caused significant health problems. Not only was there a lack of outpatient care for patients in need of medical supervision, the practice of emptying sanatoriums had resulted in a threefold increase in tuberculosis cases. Thus, by the end of September 1939, civilian medical and nursing services had descended into a state of chaos.

Nevertheless, although senior doctors and nurses were aware of hospital staffing difficulties and organisational shortcomings, the average probationer nurse seemed to be quite unaware of both government and nursing politics. Monica Dickens, recalling her wartime experience as a probationer nurse, was quite astonished by the insular nature of nurse training:

> Most of them [nurses] had no interest in anything that happened a yard outside the iron railings. They never read a paper, except the *Nursing Times*, and only turned on the Common Room wireless when the nine o'clock news was safely over. They were only interested in

the war as far as it affected them personally – shortage of Dettol and cotton wool perhaps, or jam for tea only once a week. The ward beds had ear phones fitted to them, connected with a central receiving set, and while I was dusting lockers I used to enquire about the seven o'clock news. 'Why do you always ask if there's any news?' a patient asked me one morning. 'Well, I don't know – because I'm interested I suppose.' 'Funny' she said, 'I shouldn't have thought a nurse would be interested.' That summed up the attitude of the outside world towards nurses and of nurses to the outside world. Nurse Donavon once asked me, 'Whatever were you talking to Sister Mason about at dinner?' 'Oh, the war,' I said vaguely. 'Settling world politics.'

'Good gracious,' she said, 'hadn't you got anything better to talk about than that?' I asked her what she would talk about when a German officer swaggered through the glass doors to take over the ward. 'I'd ask him if he'd had his bowels open,' she said, and laughed coarsely.[7]

In fairness to young probationers, work schedules were gruelling and they had little time with which to acquaint themselves with current affairs. They were allowed one day off a week, and were expected to attend lectures during their off-duty hours. Some, like probationer nurse Dickens, took a satirical approach to their education:

The lectures were on hygiene, nursing, anatomy and physiology. Hygiene was alright if you happened to be keen on sewage and activated sludge. A knowledge of plumbing is apparently essential to a good nurse and soon I could not pass a house without gauging the efficiency of its outside pipe system. Nursing was mostly practical work – bandaging each other and making the bed of a lay figure that was known as Old Mother Riley and appeared to be a maternity case.

Anatomy was fascinating. I started to write a story entitled: The Skeleton in the Cupboard, in which the hero was called Pyloric Sphincter and the heroine Hernia Bistoury. There was a beautiful spy called Vena Cava and a will-o-the-wisp creature called Poly O Myelitis, who led a gypsy life on a Cavernous Sinus. The heroine's unattractive friend, who was always tagging along as an unwanted third, was Ulna Tuberosity, and there was a dapper old gentleman called Sir Glenoid Fossa, who collected antiques and owned the inlaid ivory Malleolus, the blunt instrument that silenced the barking of Hernia's faithful Mastoid.[8]

In an attempt to protect their free time, probationers who were less committed to the nursing profession became adept at the art of subterfuge. The invention of sick parents or grandparents, the last-minute conjuring up of funerals of dead aunts and uncles, a fantasy catalogue of dental appointments and a series of imaginary family crises, were all introduced to unsuspecting nurse tutors as a way of avoiding lectures. Consequently, probationers who were more conscientious became extremely popular when examinations were looming large, as shirkers avidly sought their company in a desperate attempt to acquire knowledge.

New recruits, however, were more concerned with how to assimilate into the nursing hierarchy and learn the process of practical nursing. Rose Evans, a new probationer at The London in the autumn of 1939, wrote to her aunt in Wales to describe her first impressions of hospital life:

Dear Aunt Flo,

Well here I am at the famous London hospital and I can hardly believe it. Although I must admit I've blotted my copybook already. In my rush to get here I forgot the key to my suitcase and a big surly porter was summoned to force it open. He was very unhappy about being called away from his tea break to do such a thing. I could tell by the way he looked at me that he thought me far too stupid to be a nurse. I am meant to be sharing my bed room with another probationer called Gladys Tyler, but I haven't met her yet. Apparently her father is very sick. Our room is a good size with a huge oak wardrobe that almost touches the ceiling. There is also a dressing table, two beds and a desk. Wash rooms are along the corridor and a small laundry. All our uniforms are washed and pressed by the hospital laundry so we've only to wash our smalls and personal things. The food here is very stodgy. A second year called Mabel says that big chunks of bread are served with every meal. They also serve something called 'hooray pie.' It's supposed to be a meat pie but it's mainly made of potato – so if one of us manages to find some meat we are told to shout hooray.

My uniform is quite fetching but my black stockings are very thick and uncomfortable. My legs itch every time I pull them on, and to make matters worse, my flat lace up shoes make me look just like Granny.

London looks very eerie when evening comes because every building is blacked out. All our windows are crisscrossed with sticky tape to protect us from bomb blasts, and every floor has a large cupboard jam packed with iron beds ready for air raid casualties. Mabel thinks they're a waste of time. She says we're all done for – but I get the feeling she's not the most cheerful of souls! Most of our staff and patients have gone to the countryside, and there's been an awful commotion over some patients who went from St Mary's to Harefield last week – they've all gone down with meningitis.[9]

Every hospital seems to have a set of unwritten rules and The London is no different. Nurses and sisters eat on separate tables and we have to stand up every time a registered nurse comes into the dining room. Even second and third year probationers do not sit with the first years. We are the lowliest of the low and given the crummiest of jobs, like collecting sputum trays and cleaning the sluice. We have to be on the wards by 7am and we finish at 8.30pm. If we're not too busy we can have a couple of hours off in the day. Every morning at 6am I am woken by a very loud knock on the bedroom door. This is followed by a lot of door banging along the corridor as probationers go in and out of wash rooms. As you know I've never been much of an early bird and it takes me at least ten minutes to come to. My feet ache most days and my hands go bright red when I Dettol the baths. But everyone is in the same boat.

You will be pleased to know that I remembered to pack my white gloves for church, and my anatomy book for lessons, which I almost forgot because it had disappeared out of sight under my bed as I was packing. Mother calls me scatter brained. These days she's fretting about something all the time, and has taken to scrubbing the doorstep several times a day. I swear we have the shiniest front step on the Barking Road. I hope Uncle David's arthritis isn't playing up. Mother says it's down to the damp Welsh air. I have to go to dinner now – more bread and dripping! I don't know when I will see you next but I promise to write again soon.

Rose x

Just over 2 miles away, sitting in a dilapidated house on Poplar High Street, Rose's absent roommate Gladys Tyler was drinking sickly sweet sherry. Dutifully talking to some aged relatives, most of whom she could only vaguely remember from childhood, she surveyed the crowded parlour. Her father's funeral had been a straightforward, no-nonsense affair, but it seemed as though all of Poplar had turned out to say their farewells. Grief-stricken and fighting back tears, her mother sat near the window in an armchair that had clearly seen better days. Her two younger sisters, meanwhile, moved effortlessly across the dimly lit room exchanging polite pleasantries and shaking hands with mourners. Everyone agreed, as they munched their way through a mountain of sandwiches, that it had been a 'good send-off'. Gladys wondered if there could ever be a 'bad send-off'. For as long as she could remember, her father had suffered from a weak heart, the legacy of childhood rheumatic fever. She desperately wanted the day to be over, if only to escape the endless well-meaning platitudes and sympathetic glances. With a pang of guilt she took comfort from the fact that probationer nurses had to live in during their training. A ruling which gave her the perfect excuse to leave home. Overwhelmed by grief, she clutched at her sherry glass as though it were a lifeline, and walked slowly across the room to sit beside her mother. Eventually, as the afternoon drew to a close, her mother forced a smile and thanked their guests for coming. Two days later, Gladys, her compassionate leave at an end, returned to The London to restart her nurse training.

Arriving at the nurses' home, she fumbled for her keys and unlocked the bedroom door. Clearly someone else had taken up residence. There was a faint smell of gardenia in the air. Pots of cold cream and rouge lay neatly on the left-hand side of the dressing table, along with a powder compact, a string of beads and a framed photograph. Part of the imposing wardrobe was occupied by a silvery grey jacket, three cotton blouses and two skirts. Nightclothes were carefully folded on the bed nearest the sash window. Gladys, still reeling from the loss of her father, slowly unpacked her belongings and changed into her uniform. Briefly inspecting her appearance in the full length mirror, she adjusted her overly starched white cap and apron. Then, determined to seek solace in her work, she walked briskly along an empty corridor towards Matron's office to report for duty.

Matron Reynolds had just completed her daily ward rounds when Gladys knocked tentatively on her door. Amiable and efficient, she briskly called out 'Enter' then greeted her nurse with a kindly smile. Talking softly to Gladys in a reassuring manner about her father's demise, she passed her a small, crisp piece of paper. Gladys meekly accepted the handwritten duty rota, acknowledging inwardly the importance of her work – a lifeline which offered some much-needed structure and purpose. Dark, hollow shadows, etched under her eyes, were the only outward signs of her bereavement. She kept a firm lid on her emotions during the day, but cried silent tears every night before falling asleep. Vivid images of her father haunted her dreams, and flitted uninvited into her waking mind at random. Unnerved and at times overwhelmed by grief, she searched endlessly, fruitlessly for an anchor. Anything that would keep the gut-wrenching pain of loss at bay.

Matron Reynolds also understood that Gladys needed to lose herself in work. Matron was no stranger to sadness. A vast array of nursing experiences had taught her how to cope with loss. Although making the seemingly unbearable bearable was no easy task. One of her own ward sisters had soothed a bereaved husband by saying: 'Sometimes people simply have to put one foot in front of the other every day until the pain eases. Until happy memories take root inside.' Matron was heartened by her empathetic staff, and uplifted by the human ability to heal. In her youth, she had read works by ancient philosophers and was consoled by Plato's belief that philosophy provided a medical cure for souls in distress. She also expressed sympathy for those in despair and fleeing persecution. Adding a number of refugee nurses to her register, she made small comments in margins alongside these entries. For instance, writing about one young probationer nurse, who was eventually nicknamed Hockey, she noted: 'Lisbeth Hochsinger of Jewish extraction, born in Graz Austria, a medical refugee: her family have suffered greatly at the hands of the Nazis.'[10]

Lisbeth had been hurriedly brought over to England by Quakers and was a highly intelligent young woman. In her homeland she had been in the process of studying to become a doctor, when Hitler's relentless persecution of Jews had forced her to become a refugee. Upon her arrival in London, Lisbeth was informed that it was impossible for her to continue her studies, and she was encouraged to enter the nursing profession. As such, she chose to train at The London, simply because she was an excellent swimmer and the hospital boasted a good size swimming pool.

Matron Reynolds was also an intelligent woman and was known as a liberal amongst her peers. She had trained at The London, and worked as a medical research assistant before becoming a member of the Rockefella travelling fellowship. She gave unequivocal support to those who advocated improvements to technical nurse training and employed well-qualified nurse tutors. Under her excellent leadership, the title probationer nurse was changed to that of student nurse, and she prepared her nurses as much as possible for the exigencies of war.

Notes
1   Titmuss, R., *Problems of Social Policy* (1950), p. 15.
2   Staff at voluntary hospitals were subjected to the jurisdiction of the Ministry of Health from 1938 onwards. A government White Paper was published in July 1939, which outlined the Emergency Hospital Scheme and system of first aid posts. For a more in-depth analysis of emergency

medical preparations, please see National Archive Ministry of Health records: M.H./76/137, M.H.76/127 and M.H.76/348.

3 Hansard House of Commons Parliamentary Debates, 5th series, 13 June 1940, col. 1456. Debate between members of the Supply Committee and the Ministry of Health War Services.

4 'Hospital Emergency Schemes', *Nursing Illustrated*, 25 August 1939, p. 2.

5 *British Journal of Nursing*, September 1939, p. 226.

6 *Nursing Illustrated*, September 1939. Government statement appeals especially to married and retired nurses.

7 Dickens, M., *One Pair of Feet* (1942), p. 37.

8 *Ibid.*, p. 33.

9 In 1939, Harefield Sanatorium was designated as Harefield Emergency Hospital and served as a base for St Mary's Hospital. Soon after the first transfer of patients from St Mary's Hospital to Harefield in September 1939, there was an outbreak of meningococcal meningitis. All patients were treated with a relatively new drug called sulphanilamide and nobody died during this epidemic. Before the introduction of this drug, mortality rates were often as high as 90 per cent.

10 Matron Mabel Reynolds. *The London Hospital Nurses' Register*, 1939. Lisbeth Hochsinger became known by the nickname Hockey. In Austria she had been a third-year medical student until Nazi persecution threatened her family. Brought to England by Quakers, Hockey studied English language and began nurse training at The London. An extremely intelligent lady with a gift for conducting research, she eventually became director of the first Nurse Research Unit in Britain, based at Edinburgh University. Lisbeth Hockey was awarded the OBE and died in 2004.

2

THE PHONEY WAR

A mere 4 miles away via Commercial Road, Matron Gladys Verena Hillyers sat in her elegant office at St Thomas' Hospital studying the Ministry of Health's list of sector allocations, which were as follows:

Sectors one and two – The London and Essex hospitals
Sector three – St Bartholomew's and the Royal Free hospitals
Sector four – University College and Charing Cross hospitals
Sector five – The Middlesex hospital
Sector six – St Mary's hospital
Sector seven – St George's and the Westminster hospitals
Sector eight – St Thomas' hospital
Sector nine – King's College hospital
Sector ten – Guy's hospital

Below this list lay another, more complex geographical layout, which outlined the various country hospitals and territories assigned to each sector. These were the institutions responsible for admitting evacuated London patients and were staffed by the major London hospitals to which they were attached.

A petite matron, Hillyers, surrounded by floor to ceiling bookshelves, which seemed to be creaking under the weight of huge encyclopaedia-style tomes of medical and nursing knowledge, was beginning to wonder whether all of this planning was necessary. Christmas was fast approaching and there was no sign of the predicted air raids. She picked up her slightly crumpled newspaper and scanned its pages intently. Apparently more casualties were being admitted to hospitals nationwide as a result of civil defence measures. Pedestrian fatalities, for instance, had increased eightfold as a result of blackout conditions. Furthermore, it seemed that most of the murmuring of Londoner's complaints at this time centred on overzealous Air Raid Precaution (ARP) wardens, who, in their efforts to ensure neighbourhoods adhered strictly to the blackout, issued hefty fines to those who failed to comply. Even the furnaces of the Royal Society for the Protection of Animals (RSPCA) had to be drenched with water to prevent flickering embers from lighting the London skyline. This was becoming increasingly difficult as thousands of people queued up to have their pets destroyed. According to matron's newspaper, over a million cats and dogs were put down between September and December 1939. Mainly because pets were not allowed to enter public air raid shelters, and owners considered it a kindness to end their pets' lives rather than subject them to air raids. Keepers at London Zoo had also been forced to destroy all poisonous snakes and spiders in case these escaped during bombing raids.

Matron Hillyers, trying not to dwell on this macabre fact, decided to make one final review of St Thomas' preparations for air raid casualties. An emergency committee, which included herself, the house governor, surveyors and senior surgeons, had formulated clear plans for the reception of casualties and for the protection of the hospital. Fire was the biggest risk to the hospital, so firefighting teams, consisting of porters and medical students, were organised to deal with this problem. A triage system was introduced for trauma victims, which included a clinical reception room, specially equipped wards and basement operating theatres. Medical students were assigned as stretcher bearers and wound dressers, and there were designated medical teams to organise blood transfusions. White rabbits were also painted on the walls of basement corridors to help medical personnel negotiate the myriad of underground passageways. With the exception of white rabbits, similar preparations were put in place at The London Hospital. Additional electricity generators were purchased in readiness for interrupted power supplies, and extra water tanks installed to ensure access to clean water. London was well prepared for the predicted onslaught of terrifying proportions.

However, Christmas came and went with still no sign of bombs. Londoners began to relax, many even forgetting to take their gas masks to work. Hospitals reopened their outpatient departments and gradually retrieved some of their staff and medical equipment from the country.

In the meantime, Matron Hillyers, along with other matrons such as Mabel Reynolds at The London, made every effort to keep in touch with their scattered nurse training schools in the countryside. This was no easy task, as one sister from The London confided to the *Nurses' League Review*:

> In some cases the units were left entirely alone, in others they were just added to the present staff of the hospital. This arrangement was not so satisfactory, because their methods of administration were so very different from our own. As a result it became very difficult to carry on with the training of our nurses, as so often they were not working under London Hospital sisters, but, of course, that like everything else, had to be overlooked until the initial emergency was over.[1]

Moreover, there were more than a few disgruntled probationer nurses. Florence Johnson, known to her friends and family as Flo, was in training at St Thomas' and wrote to her parents from Guildford:

Dear Mum and Dad,

I hope everything is chipper where you are. Things here are exceedingly tedious. We are bored to tears! Yesterday we spent nearly all day bandaging chair legs and cleaning cupboards. We are waiting for casualties that never come and working in an old mental asylum. None of us are happy. The surrounding countryside is very beautiful but we are completely isolated. There is only one bus into the village a week. We tried to organize a dance last Saturday night but the only musical instrument for miles is the church organ. An old grounds-man called Fred told us he can play a few good tunes using just some old saucepans and spoons, but we decided to abandon the idea of a dance altogether.

The food here is awful and the last meal is served at 4pm! Our uniforms are hanging off us and I'd give anything for some jam roly poly and custard. There are rumours that we might be moved back to London soon … we can but hope.

Your affectionate daughter

Flo x

Flo's best friend Grace Davies had similar complaints, writing to her brother of 'endless bread and dripping and tasteless soup'.

Problems associated with countryside sector hospitals were numerous. Aside from their isolated locations and weak transport links, none of them were geared up to take air raid casualties. Most were old sanatoriums and mental asylums. Many were overrun with rats and cockroaches. When one ward sister complained about filthy kitchens and hundreds of mice, a hospital porter gave her a large black and white cat as a solution. Furthermore, such institutions lacked both the necessary equipment and functional operating theatres. Even when makeshift operating theatres were established and equipment upgraded, conditions left a lot to be desired. Staff at these local authority hospitals were often poorly trained, demotivated and under resourced. Within a matter of weeks, newly installed staff from London hospitals became aware of the wide financial chasm which existed between voluntary and municipal hospitals. As Dr Clark-Kennedy of The London noted:

Everyone had been suddenly jolted out of the normal routine of his existence. Voluntary and county council hospitals had got mixed up together. Staff and students had seen for themselves the neglected holes and corners of medical organization of the country, particularly problems of the aged and chronic sick with which the county council hospitals and public assistance institutions remained under a statutory obligation to deal and which the voluntary hospitals had so far successfully avoided.[2]

During this period of calm before the storm which became known as the Phoney War, the funds of voluntary hospitals were particularly buoyant:

On the financial side there was less anxiety than might have been expected. Taxation had increased with the war and voluntary subscriptions had fallen off, but the consequences of that had been more than offset by the now much decreased cost of running the hospital and by money received from the Ministry for services rendered to the Emergency Medical Scheme. The latter included payment for maintaining casualty beds and the board of all London Hospital lay staff working at sector hospitals. The financial year ended with a credit balance of £2000![3]

Great Ormond Street Hospital (GOSH) was also financially solvent at this time and received three anonymous donations in just one day: £33 10s from someone whose birthday fell on 1 August, £2,000 'from a friend' and £1,000 from a provincial friend who had recently visited the hospital.[4]

Designated a casualty clearing station, GOSH was also experiencing a quiet time, although hospital life was reasonably normal. Only 47 per cent of English city children had been evacuated to the countryside and over 90 per cent of these had returned to cities by December 1939.

However, in April 1940, just as London County Council began reopening schools for returning evacuees, the Phoney War came to an abrupt end. Britain was defeated in its Norwegian campaign. There followed a rapid chain of events that shocked the populations of both Britain and her closest ally, France. On 10 May, Germans invaded the

Netherlands, Belgium and Luxembourg. Neville Chamberlain resigned
as British Prime Minister and was replaced by Winston Churchill. On
12 May, the Germans put paid to the idea that they were only interested
in expanding eastwards and crossed the border into France. As German
tanks advanced towards northern France, the British Expeditionary
Force beat a hasty retreat and became trapped at Dunkirk. Here, nearly
400,000 British and French soldiers, under constant aerial bombardment
and artillery fire, waited to be rescued. Urgent government radio appeals
brought an immediate response from the British maritime community
and a flotilla of 900 ships, many privately owned, bravely set sail for
Dunkirk. Between 26 May and 4 June they ferried almost 340,000
troops back to Britain.

Military nurse Colonel Margaret Kneebone was on duty in France at
this time, and recalled:

We had gone over to Dieppe around the middle of May. We arrived
at five in the evening and suddenly there was an air raid warning and
bombs dropping all around. I was taking a shower at the time. We had to
take our tin hats with us everywhere and I came out in my vest and tin
hat. However, they didn't hit us and I couldn't believe that they would.

It was crowded and it was the first time I had seen battle exhaustion.
It was a pathetic sight. Their faces were blue, and they were just too
tired to move. However, we got to a station and someone said 'Do you
want a cup of tea?' So we sat over there and they had enormous crates
of stores and the French people were looting like mad.

We got the order to take no more patients. So I went to my Red
Cross store and I got an enormous amount of supplies: mittens, socks,
gloves and everything else. I gathered them up and thought the
Germans shan't have these, and I went and gave them to the orderlies
and anybody else who wanted them. Then just about midday whilst
I was in the quartermaster's store a company officer, a very smart
territorial, came to the door, saluted me and said, 'Madam, the order
has come, immediate movement, get into the ambulances and get
outside the door. You cannot go to the billets and get your things. As

you have had your lunch and we haven't, go to your store cupboard and gather up all the tinned food you can and as quickly as you can …' But there were four of my sisters down at the billet having lunch. Not one of them said a word. I brought them up on words, not to question why, yours but to do or die!

For days and nights, ships of all kinds plied to and fro across the channel under the fierce onslaught of the enemy's bombers. As each ship came in, the army doctors at the port would shout out to the Captain on the bridge to ask for the number of wounded, and in a few minutes the ambulances and stretchers would be alongside to bring them off and take them to the waiting hospital trains in the station. The organization of the port was excellent. The ships were being unloaded at an astonishing speed and no sooner were they empty than they were disappearing through the harbour entrance back to France to fetch more men home.[5]

Throughout the Dunkirk retreat, which Churchill described as a 'miracle of deliverance', British and French troops flowed steadily into the safety of English ports. Thus the first victims of war to be nursed in London sector hospitals were not the expected air raid victims from London but a mixture of British and French soldiers from the Dunkirk evacuation. However, for nurses who had languished for months in sector hospitals bandaging chair legs and doing menial cleaning work, the Dunkirk retreat was a welcome relief from their suffocating boredom. At last there was an opportunity to do some real nursing.

Writing to her parents, Flo described the wounded:

The men are suffering from severe exhaustion, gun shot and shrapnel wounds. Their nerves are torn to shreds and look like quivering wrecks. Many have nightmares and are extremely agitated. Most do not want to talk about anything at all, they simply grunt or nod when you do things for them. Sister says they are in shock. But there is a young Private who talks to me. He tells me every morning when I give him his breakfast that as soon as he shuts his eyes he can see the dead bodies of his friends floating in the sea around him … their eyes glazed over. He says the sea was deep red with blood, and the deafening sound of machine guns, aircraft and explosions horrific. One of his friends was literally thrown onto a boat over the side of the pier. He landed very heavily on the deck with an almighty thud, but he was alright and survived to tell the tale. When the men were first bedded down on the wards there was a very strong smell of alcohol … sister says that the men ran out of antiseptics so wounds were liberally doused with French brandy to ward off infection. I think they must have used hundreds of bottles because they stank to high heaven.

Grace Davies also wrote about the sudden influx of military patients, but was most enamoured with the improvements in conditions that had accompanied them:

Since the arrival of troops food supplies have been stepped up enormously and lorry loads are arriving at least three times a week. Cooked meals are served to the troops four times a day. The last meal is supper and it is served at 8pm. We have more meat and eggs. When the men first got here we nurses still had to have our last meal at 4pm, but sister tutor had a word with the M. O. and he agreed that we can have the same meals and meal times as the men. It's made a world of difference to us. I have far more energy now and find I sleep much easier than I did on an empty stomach.

For the thousands of men who were hastily and bravely plucked from Dunkirk, the trip across the Channel was undoubtedly uncomfortable. The bedraggled walking wounded shuffled through the ports, barely acknowledging their surroundings. Others, with gaping wounds covered in blood-soaked blankets, were carefully carried by stretcher bearers. They were all tired, dirty and despondent. But at least they were safe. Over 40,000 British troops did not make it back. They were either brutally killed or taken prisoner. These included members of the 51st Highland Brigade, who had been fighting strenuous rearguard battles, in order to allow many others an opportunity to escape. Royal Army Medical Corps (RAMC) personnel had also been told to hold the line and remain with severely wounded men.

As Germany forcefully pursued its Blitzkrieg policy across Europe, there was little in the way of resistance. On 10 June, Italy entered the fray on the side of Germany, declaring war on Britain and France. By 14 June, the Germans had taken over France and gained control of Paris. The frail French leader Marshal Pétain was 82 years old and had little emotional or physical strength with which to fight the Nazis. He surrendered France to Germany almost immediately, and formed an official government in Vichy in central France.

A stoical Churchill spoke of the Dunkirk evacuation in heroic terms, but also admitted that wars could not be won by evacuations. Subsequently, in his famous 'we will fight them on the beaches and never surrender' speech, he gave the British people stark warnings of what was to come. He also issued a Cromwellian alert, which indicated that an invasion of Britain was highly likely in the next twenty-four hours. With the fall of France, Britain and its Empire stood alone against the threat of Nazi expansion. Moreover, the success of Germany's Blitzkrieg policy and the rapid capitulation of France had imbued the Nazis with a heightened confidence. Indeed, Hermann Göring, Commander-in-Chief of the Luftwaffe, believed the Nazis to be invincible. However, Hitler's Blitzkrieg policy relied on lightning-fast strikes and rapidly moving forces; and no amount of German Panzer divisions could reach Britain without crossing the sea. Therefore, in order to implement Operation Sea Lion, the German code name for Hitler's proposed invasion of Britain, Göring's Luftwaffe needed to subdue the British Royal Navy and Royal Air Force (RAF). The subsequent and crucial air battle between the RAF and the Luftwaffe began on 10 July. It became known as the Battle of Britain, and was unique in being the first battle to be decided by air power alone.

Furthermore, the aftermath of Dunkirk highlighted for many the reality of war. It also stirred up considerable animosity towards refugees living in Britain. Rumours abounded of subversive behaviour amongst groups of refugees, with sometimes ludicrous accusations of criminal intent. A sense of paranoia infiltrated even the most sensible of communities and nursing was no exception. Prompted by a shortage of nurses, the Ministry of Health had initially pleaded with matrons to employ refugee nurses from Austria, Germany and Eastern Europe, but there was now a backlash and a questioning of government policy in this respect. Articles in the nursing press approached the issue with considerable fervour:

> The inevitable war was declared, and thus a very difficult situation in connection with foreign probationers has arisen in hospitals which admitted these refugees in the first instance, with very little enquiry or supervision. In our opinion the whole scheme was wrong – it would now seem advisable that it should cease until peace is declared.
>
> Great Britain is a small island, and there is neither further space nor food for more groups of foreigners of which thousands have been admitted within the past year. Austrians, Poles, Belgians, Dutch and French people are to be met in London – men, women and children. The question of work must naturally arise, let us hope it can be found, as idle people are unhappy people. It is to be hoped that the Americas will make an effort to admit more emigrants than the law at present provides – Great Britain has been generous to a fault – let the rest of the world, at least, help the needy, if it is unable to fight to prevent further indigence.[6]

Even matrons of relatively small hospitals became reluctant to admit refugee girls for nurse training courses. Writing to the Board of Governors of Royal Waterloo Hospital, Matron Ruth Clarkson pointed out: 'We have in all four alien refugees in training. As we are still getting enough applications from British girls to keep up our numbers, I do not feel that we should have a larger proportion of foreigners.'[7]

Ministry of Health officials, proving they were not entirely immune to the waves of paranoia sweeping the country, eventually reached a compromise. All refugee nurses were henceforth known as aliens and were not allowed to work on male wards, or come into contact with members of the armed forces. A Ministry of Health circular issued orders to this effect. Nevertheless, not all matrons complied with these official instructions. Some insisted that some experience of nursing men was a vital component of nurse training, whilst others flouted regulations because of staff shortages. These matrons often became the target of snide insinuations from other staff members. A porter at The London, for instance, was quite convinced that Matron arranged her washing on a line on the hospital roof in a certain fashion, in order to send messages to enemy aircraft.[8] Government propaganda posters with cartoon drawings of Hitler hiding behind trees as groups of evacuated children picnicked in the countryside, and listening in as people chatted innocently on buses, accompanied by captions such as 'careless talk costs lives', did nothing to abate the wartime paranoia in hospitals. If someone appeared to have extra rations or luxury goods, they easily fell under the suspicion of fellow workers. Fuelled by the national and nursing press, unfounded allegations of colluding with the enemy became more frequent and exaggerated as the war progressed. Even an innocent BBC interpreter, who was evacuated to Evesham for safety, was arrested by local police for behaving oddly, and for speaking a foreign language.

Rose, who was very fond of refugee nurse Hockey, was indignant on her behalf:

> I don't understand what all the fuss is about. Hockey is classed as an Alien yet she is an excellent worker, very witty and fun to be around. To think she might harm one of her patients is just too ridiculous for words. Mind you she does have a tendency to speak her mind, and is not at all fearful of the sisters. Actually we need more nurses like her, all this cow-towing [*sic*] to authority is not always a good thing. I do wish I had Hockey's courage to speak out when sister is in the wrong, or orders us about like we're her servants … I just mutter quietly under my breath.

According to the minutes recorded by London matrons, many shared Rose's opinion, a few even admitted to throwing Ministry of Health circulars straight in the bin without even looking at them. In some respects they could be forgiven for doing so, because Ministry of Health circulars fell on their desks like autumn leaves. Moreover, the problem of supervising nurses and domestic staff in London and sector hospitals left matrons little time to read everything in detail. One nurse described Christmas in a sector hospital, which had previously been a workhouse:

> We were horrified really because we found that the people who were there were unmarried mothers or fallen girls, the poor, the elderly and tramps. There were tramps' wards, casual wards and there were cells for drunks who could be picked up and put there. But the building we were in was reasonable.
>
> We spent Christmas there. The matron of this workhouse wanted to give us a nice Christmas Day and we had quite a nice first course. Then the Christmas pudding was brought in, aflame, how marvellous. We said 'how lovely', Christmas pudding and we all tackled it, and we discovered that it had been set alight by methylated spirits – which was awful. But we felt we had had Christmas Day in the workhouse![9]

Notes

1 *The Royal London Hospital Nurses' League Review*, nos ix and x (1940–41) p. 19.
2 Clark-Kennedy, A.E., *London Pride: the Story of a Voluntary Hospital* (1979), pp. 215–16. During the first full year of the war the income of The London exceeded expenditure by over £40,000.
3 *Ibid.*, p. 215.
4 *British Journal of Nursing*, August 1939, p. 216.
5 Colonel Margaret Kneebone oral history testimony: Starns, P., *Frontline Females*, BBC Radio 4, 1998.
6 *British Journal of Nursing*, October 1940, p. 175.
7 London Metropolitan Archives, ref: H01/RW/C/01/003, Matron's report book: entry dated 3 September 1940.
8 *The Royal London Hospital Nurses' League Review*, nos ix and x (1940–41), p. 19.
9 *Frontline Females*, vol. 1.

3

THE FIRST NIGHT
OF THE BLITZ

The Battle of Britain was still raging above the English Channel when the London Blitz began. It was a warm, sunny, cloudless afternoon on Saturday, 7 September 1940. Londoners were leisurely going about their business – picnicking in parks, strolling through busy streets, attending matinee performances at theatres and cinemas – when the air raid warning siren signalled incoming German bombers at 16.43 hours. Guided by the River Thames, they flew like an ominous swarm of giant crane flies towards London's industrial heartland. Within an hour, the whole of London's East End was ablaze. Incendiary bombs fell like meteor showers across factories, industrial warehouses and the docks. These started fires which further guided the bombers to their targets, then high-explosive bombs landed on both sides of the River Thames with terrifying crashes and thunderous noise. Like a violent earthquake, the ground shook and buildings split and shattered under the onslaught of aerial bombardment. Horrific fires engulfed the Ford motor factory at Dagenham, West and East India Docks, and Woolwich. Streets were swarming with rats trying to escape bombed-out factories and warehouses, and East End rail links were completely destroyed. Beckton gasworks received a direct hit, disrupting power supplies across the city.

Dead and injured people were blasted onto the roofs of buildings and vehicles. At 18.30 hours, the bombers turned to head back to their airfields in France, then a mere two hours later a further harrowing onslaught began, an intense air raid that continued throughout the night. An Australian surgeon working in London that night described the scene:

> I'll never forget that hectic first night. At half past eleven my phone rang. I was wanted at the hospital urgently. It's only two or three minutes' walk, but how brightly the streets and buildings were lit by the glow of a huge fire! There just wasn't a black out any longer, and bombs were dropping all over the place.
>
> At hospital, stretcher cases were coming in. A bomb had dropped near the entrance of a cinema not far away. It was just at the end of the show when people were crowding the footpath. Many were killed and wounded. So the war had started at last, but what an odd collection of wounded. Women and children, soldiers on leave, firemen, a bus driver and his ticket collector, and two waitresses going home from work. I asked one woman: 'Did you hear the bomb coming down?' She said, 'Coo, did I ear it! I'll say I did, and I lie strite down in the gutter.' She was lucky; only slight injuries of the hand.
>
> A Canadian soldier, on whom I later operated, was very disgruntled. He'd been over here all year waiting to have a go at the Jerrys, and now his bomb wound was to keep him out of action for a long time. A British Tommy was indignant; passing unharmed through Dunkirk, he'd been bombed in his native London, first time on leave.[1]

The British Tommy was Archie Foster. He had been out on a first date with Nurse Flo. Archie had met Flo earlier in the year, whilst a patient at the sector hospital where she worked. They had exchanged several letters and arranged to meet up during his first period of leave. Along with other sector hospital nurses, Flo had been recalled to London in the summer to boost staffing levels, because city hospitals had increased the number of ordinary civilian beds. Like most young girls, Flo had eagerly awaited the arrival of her sweetheart's leave. Blue eyed, with flaxen-coloured hair and babyish facial features, she had dressed carefully in a pale blue cotton print dress, adorned with a daisy-shaped brooch. She had walked to the cinema to meet her beau in the autumn sunshine and they had found discreet seats near the back row of the cinema. They watched the most popular film of the day – *Gone with the Wind* – and the newsreels, before stepping back out into the sunshine. They heard the siren, but had no time to seek shelter. A bomb came whizzing down, shaking the road, pavement and concrete buildings. Archie had instantly dived on top of Florence to protect her from the blast. In doing so, he sustained three fractures and a gaping wound to his arm and shoulder. Florence was badly shaken but physically unhurt.

Archie was luckier than most, as the Australian surgeon continued:

Some of the injuries were horrible. I will not go into the grim details. But I do want you to know of the brave and uncomplaining spirit in which these Londoners accepted their wounds. There was no weeping, no hysteria, and no panic. Many were the gallant deeds that night. None were braver than the firemen and the rescue parties.

Not long after the start of blitzkrieg I was in the middle of an operation, extracting a bomb fragment from a man's arm, when the air was pierced by the now familiar whistle of a falling bomb. It shrieked, closer and closer. There was a terrific explosion. It had fallen just outside. The hospital shook and rattled. After a moment's silence, someone said: 'Rotten shots, these miserable Huns.'

For a moment we were not greatly upset. That came a minute or two later when the lights in the operating theatre went down to a low glow, flickered and then went out altogether. Still, an electric torch was quickly shone on the wound and the work went on. In a minute or two our emergency electrical circuit came into action and the lights were on again. We operated continually all that night. The 'all clear' came about six o'clock. Still we remained, half expecting a fresh influx of casualties when daylight made search possible among the wreckage. It speaks volumes for the work of the rescue parties in the blackout that when morning came no new patient was brought to us. After a cup of tea and a biscuit we went to the roof of the hospital to survey the damage. After the noise and fury of that night frankly I expected to see half of London in ruins, but there it was, apparently unharmed. Big Ben struck seven o'clock in unhurried and unconcerned tones. That was a solid reassurance from the very heart of the Empire.[2]

Elsewhere that night, a high-explosive bomb fell on the ward kitchens of 'I' block of New Cross Hospital. Four nurses who were drinking their tea in the kitchens at the time were killed instantly, and a night sister in the ward was injured along with some of her patients. Nurse Sole, who was also in the kitchen when the bomb struck, was propelled through a rapidly disintegrating floor into a corridor beneath. A 44-year-old porter named Albert Dolphin hurriedly went to her assistance and found her pinned to the spot by a huge block of masonry, which covered her legs from her thighs to her ankles. He and a small party of men worked frantically to release her, but as they worked the wall split and caved in on top of them. The rescue workers quickly managed to extricate themselves before the wall crumbled, but Dolphin chose to remain and threw himself on top of Nurse Sole, saving her life in the process. Dolphin died as a result of his instinctive act of bravery and was posthumously awarded the George Cross.

As hospitals worked under pressure to tend to the injured, off-duty nurses and medical staff rushed to help their colleagues. A deluge of casualties streamed through hospital doors. Kathleen Raven was one of the nurses on duty at St Bartholomew's Hospital:

> Bart's was hit that night. I was caring for casualties on the first floor of the new block when I was blown right across the ward, the blast taking the window and all before it. I was unhurt. Hundreds of casualties were brought to us that night, the theatres worked non-stop and the nurses and doctors worked together day and night. We patched up the charred and broken bodies and as soon as they were fit to move we saw them off to Hill End on the Green Line ambulances.[3]

Flo, who had earlier accompanied Archie to hospital, subsequently picked her way through the fallen debris to the nurses' home. The streets were brightly lit by huge flickering flames, and great palls of black smoke covered the whole area. Once at St Thomas' nurses' home, Flo quickly donned her uniform and rushed to the casualty department. Still shaken from her earlier traumatic experience, she attempted to behave as though nothing untoward was happening:

> I felt as though I were numb, almost as though time had stood still. I had narrowly escaped a bomb and only hours later I was on duty. There was a dreadful noise and everyone was rushing about getting bandages, antiseptics and dressings but apart from the noise it was just like a very busy nightshift. We were too busy doing our work to worry about bombs. Even when the ground was shaking we remained unruffled – after all we had patients to look after. Besides sister could be a bit of a dragon and we were certain that Hitler wouldn't dare drop a bomb on her! Silly really I know. We admitted a lot of casualties. One tearful old lady was most upset because the bombing had interrupted her baking day. She just taken a fruit cake out of the oven when she was thrown to the ground by the bombardment. She had ignored the siren, thinking it was a false alarm. In her broad cockney accent she told me all the ingredients she had mixed for her cake, she was especially proud of the eggs she'd collected from chickens in her back yard, 'What this bombing all do to them laying I don't know!' Luckily she only had superficial wounds which I dressed quickly. One of our maids kindly made her a cup of cocoa because she was badly shaken up poor dear.[4]

Grace, meanwhile, had been resting in St Thomas' nurses' home when the Blitz began; she too had rushed to help her colleagues. Working tirelessly in a surgical ward throughout the night, she gave a huge sigh of relief when the all clear sounded at dawn. Emerging from the hospital corridors, she surveyed the surrounding streets. Huddles of weary humanity, stunned and bewildered, were searching for relatives and friends. An old man sat amongst the rubble with his head in his hands.

Fallen masonry and piles of shattered glass were strewn across roads and paths. Fireman were carefully picking through debris, and making piles of dead bodies on a street corner. Grace observed the scene of carnage. Fighting back empathetic tears, she undid her uniform belt and scrunched up her blood-splattered apron ready for the laundry.

In Whitechapel, The London Hospital had also been dealing with large numbers of casualties. Porters and medical students tried to evacuate as many existing patients as possible to make way for incoming wounded. They also struggled to carry all patients to the ground floors, since the amount of water used to put out fires had rendered hospital hydraulic lifts useless. Throughout the night, sisters and nurses wearing tin hats at an amusingly jaunty angle checked on patients' welfare. All had escape stories to tell, some more miraculous than others. Frank Jenkins sustained multiple fractures and a head injury, but was eager to tell his tale to Nurse Gladys Tyler as she patiently dressed his wounds:

> I took cover in Poplar when a bomb crashed on the pavvy next to us and blew the whole bloody lot in. Shelter shook – collapsed like a pack of cards. Blown right across the road I was, an pinned down by tubes [steel struts which supported the roof]. Others were screaming and hollering, a right old din going on. Then I heard gushing water and I thinks to myself, we're all for it now … we gonna drown. But we 'eard voices calling and men were moving bricks an that. We saw a lantern and thought Thank the Lord for that![5]

Gladys smiled as cheerfully as she could and uttered reassuring words to Frank. All the time, she was wondering how her mother and sisters were doing. The London had not been hit that night but she was certain that some members of her family would be worse for wear. She suspected, too, that her roommate Rose was lying injured somewhere in the vicinity. Rose had been visiting her parents on the Barking Road and nobody had seen her since Friday evening. Every available nurse, probationer or trained, had hurried to hospitals to lend a hand with casualties. The fact that Rose had not put in an appearance gave Gladys a dreadful sense of foreboding. She had not known her roommate long, but had grown to like her. Rose was a funny, vivacious character with hazel eyes and dark chestnut curly hair, which she styled to resemble Vivien Leigh's. Before the war Rose could have been described as buxom, but due to an aversion to hospital food she had become as slim as the rest of her group. Rose loved dancing and trips to the cinema, and would often go to see the same film over and over again, until she could recite most of the script by heart. Gladys was more introverted, composed, self-disciplined and thoughtful. A lifetime of caring for her invalid father before his demise had cultivated a seriousness of character that was difficult for her to shake off. Gladys longed to be cultured and sophisticated. She enjoyed classical music concerts, especially the lunchtime concerts featuring her favourite pianist, Myra Hess. As the eldest of three sisters, Gladys also believed that she needed to set an example to her siblings, one of hard work, forbearance, emotional control and steadfast endurance in the face of adversity. Rose, meanwhile, was an antidote to her self-imposed reserve, a giggling extrovert who spent time and effort trying to coax Gladys to embrace life. To date, her efforts had failed to have any impact, but the horror of bombing and witnessing the long queue of human frailty had stirred in Gladys a brief desire to emulate her roommate.

The night had been harrowing, and the stream of casualties seemingly endless. Those who had witnessed war before were compelled to vent their feelings:

A succession of ambulances arrive at the entrance to a hospital. Stretchers are taken out, placed on rubber tyre trollies and move quietly, speedily into the building. Each carries some man, woman or child from a nearby working class tenement, shattered in the first of the Hun daylight raids on London. 'This is not war' said a man, hardened to all that war used to mean. In war, as he had known it during four long years in France, men fought against men, with equal chances. This was something different. The cavalcade was certainly a sad one and in some respects sadder than those, which flowed through casualty clearing stations in France.[6]

Undoubtedly, this first sustained air raid on London signalled a different kind of warfare, and emergency services and hospitals coped as best they could. Triage systems were efficient, oxygen therapy was available to those who required it, blood transfusions for patients with severe haemorrhages and sulphonamides to treat infection. Dr Arthur Walker, a junior doctor working at St Thomas', noted:

> The morale of patients was very good. I assisted other doctors, did some stitches, cleaned up wounds and held up legs for plaster, that sort of thing. I was not shocked by the wounds and they became run of the mill. The corner of Westminster Bridge and Lambeth Palace Road was a wreck. Patients felt very strongly about the Germans but there was never any talk of giving in. The patients were reasonably cheerful, they had guts.[7]

As Gladys suspected, Rose was lying injured. Along with other family members, she had dived under the kitchen table at their home on the Barking Road when the bombing started. Surrounded by mayhem, she was knocked unconscious by falling debris and had lain for several hours before being dragged out by rescue workers; her parents had suffered minor injuries but were trapped under a pile of bricks and plaster. It took a considerable time to extricate the family. Rose was taken to a first aid post nearby, where her superficial head wound was cleansed and dressed. Eventually regaining consciousness, she was taken to her aunt's house, which thankfully was still standing. Feeling confused and slightly dizzy, the concussed Rose promptly fell asleep with her anxious mother at her bedside. There was no way of contacting matron to inform her of her daughter's whereabouts and condition. Power cables had been severed and telegraph poles brought down. Screaming, panic-stricken children searched for their parents amongst the rubble, and rescue parties worked frantically to save as many people as possible.

Emergency services were stretched to breaking point, and life for nurses working outside the hospitals was no less fraught. Rose's cousin Rhoda worked as a nursing auxiliary on number seven ambulance train:

In the station was a long train made up of cattle trucks with gutters down the middle of the floors. Commands were given and the long seats on the platform were manhandled into the coaches. All the newspapers on a kiosk were taken for use on the train. Then we were paired off with a sister. Three of the sisters had been in the First World War. Two had been sent to Siberia and Sister Barker who seemed to be in charge had served on the frontline in France.

Soon the patients from Hallam hospital began to arrive; stretcher cases, others in chairs and some walking. Sister and I had the ward with the latter and a small boy who sat on a pile of newspapers looking through a hole at the passing scene. He had never been on a train before. After the journey we ate our sandwiches. Then Sister Barker called for volunteers to shake, fold and count the blankets we had received in exchange for ours. This had to be done after every journey. We returned home very tired indeed.

Next we had to report to Monument Road station. In the sheds we found a dirty banana train which had to be scrubbed and scraped clean. We were issued with giant sized operating gowns to protect our clothing. They had to be tucked up and in by a piece of bandage round our waists. When the train was clean we were issued with our uniforms – skirts to be worn twelve inches above the ground. Thank goodness I was stock size – others had to do a lot of altering. We were promptly nicknamed the milkmaids because our caps were made of white cloth and a short length of elastic with holes in!

We were involved in the bombing of Kent Road. Having dug out three casualties and taken them to the First Aid Post, we found it had just been bombed. Sister seemed shell-shocked – the nurses who had been either side of her had been blown away; two more on the stairs had been stripped naked. My dad and another man ran to get blankets to cover them. They would not let us go downstairs even though I was in uniform and the others were first aiders. All sister wanted was a cup of tea. She looked at me as if I were a ghost, perhaps one of her nurses who had run to the next first aid post to telephone for help. I saw two nurses amongst the rubble, one was bleeding and made little movement and groaned. I bathed her face with water from one of the buckets that stood there, to stop the blood going into her eyes and mouth. I had never really smelt blood before. Three men with a stretcher came running through and kicked the water all over us. As I was soaked and thought they had come to collect the patients, I went home.[8]

On the morning of 8 September 1940, Winston Churchill toured the East End to survey the bomb damage. Over 400 people had been killed overnight, with hundreds more injured. Subsequently, London, with the exception of one night, was raided by day or night for fifty-six consecutive dates. Severe bombing continued until 10 May 1941. As dusk fell each evening, loud wailing sirens sounded an alarm, and Londoners quickly sought shelter in public or private air raid shelters. Droning incoming German planes became a familiar sound, as did the horrific bombing sprees across the city. Londoners gradually became adept at dealing with air raids and made considerable efforts to maintain a sense of normality. American journalist Quentin Reynolds observed:

Damage is incomparable to anything that has gone before. But London has the greatest civilian army ever assembled. Bank clerks and shop keepers by day become heroes by night. When the raid finishes London looks up towards the dawn and faces the day with calm, morale higher than before; a population fused together by a surging spirit of courage and determination. I am a neutral reporter. I watch Londoners live and die, but I can assure you there is no fear and panic in Churchill's island, only courage and determination. Bombs cannot kill the unconquerable spirit of the people of London.[9]

Clearly a small section of London's population did scream and panic. Many were frightened out of their wits. Furthermore, despite upbeat reports of cheerful camaraderie and expert efficiency, some problems remained. Distressing scenes of piles of dead bodies, for example, arranged like sacks on street corners, posed a significant dilemma. Hospitals refused to deal with them because they were obviously beyond medical help, and mortuaries refused to accept them without signed death certificates from a doctor. It took considerable time to speed up the process by which dead bodies were moved with a degree of dignity, to places where they could be identified by their families. A lack of air raid shelters, particularly in newly reopened schools, was also highlighted by national newspapers. Furthermore, concern over a lack of helmets for district nurses and midwives prompted *The Times* to print a direct appeal to the Ministry of Health. The *British Journal of Nursing* reported the situation:

For some time the managers of the Queen's Institute for District Nursing have been anxious that Queen's Nurses and Midwives, who have run risks on duty from raids and bombs, should be provided by the Government with steel helmets. This would appear to be a national duty for the safety of these invaluable public servants. But no; for some time as usual the Ministry of Health 'could not see its way.' Then the public and *The Times* found no difficulty in doing so. Result, the following satisfactory information from the Hon. Secretary of the Institute, in reply to a letter to the Ministry of Health.

Sir – The attention of the Queen's Institute of District Nursing has been called to a letter in *The Times* of September 5th on the subject of the provision of steel helmets for district nurses. Representations on this subject have been made to the Ministry of Health from time to time, and a circular (No. 2124) has been received from them, stating that the subject had received consideration and asking local authorities to supply particulars of the number of helmets and respirators required for midwives and also for district nurses who are not midwives. It is hoped that this need will be supplied as soon as a sufficient number of helmets is available.

Nursing associations should therefore, apply to the scheme making authorities of their county, borough or area, stating the number of midwives or district nurses employed. In the case of those associations which are affiliated to the County nursing associations, the necessary steps will doubtless be taken by County associations on their behalf.

This matter has given grave anxiety to the Queen's Institute and all responsible for the safety of midwives and district nurses, whose service to the community is now being carried on under such dangerous conditions, and we welcome the sympathetic decision of the Ministry in this urgent matter.

Yours faithfully,

D. Keville-Davies, Hon. Secretary of the Q.I.D.N., Chairman of the Midwifery Committee. Queen's Institute of District Nursing, 57, Lower Belgrave Street, S.W.1, September 6th.

Better late than never![10]

District nurses and midwives could be forgiven for being sarcastic. They had been badgering the government to supply steel helmets for almost a year, and very few had received them in time for the Blitz. It was not the first time the Ministry of Health had dragged its feet over a crucial nursing issue and it was certainly not the last. Registered nurses and midwives were constantly on their guard against charlatans and inadequate patient care, since the civilian sector of nursing was severely diluted with untrained staff, sometimes with dangerous consequences.

Notes

1   Curnock, G., *Hospitals Under Fire* (1941), pp. 105–06.
2   *Ibid.*, pp. 106–08.
3   K. Raven DBE, *Royal College of Nursing History of Nursing Journal*, vol. 3, no. 3 (1990), pp. 44–45.
4   Starns, P., *Frontline Females*, BBC Radio 4, vol. 1, 1998.
5   Tyler, Gladys, Oral history interview, 1993.
6   Curnock, *op. cit.*, (1941), p. 131.
7   Walker, A., Oral history interview, Imperial War Museum Sound Archive ref: 17977/2/1-2, reel 1.
8   Evans, R., *Royal College of Nursing History of Nursing Journal*, vol. 3, no. 3 (1990), pp. 60–63.
9   Reynolds, Q., *Britain can take it*. Film broadcast, October 1940.
10 *British Journal of Nursing*, September 1940, p. 158.

4

TAKING TO THE UNDERGROUND

In many respects, the process of shifting Luftwaffe attention away from bombing airfields onto the bombing of major cities and industrial works proved to be a German strategic error, since it afforded the Royal Air Force some respite in which to regroup, rest their pilots and consolidate. Mistakenly believing Germany to be unassailable, Göring pressed ahead with terrifying air raids across Britain. Many of these were carried out in broad daylight in an attempt to destroy British morale. In the first raid alone, 200 bombers wreaked havoc across London.

Matrons Hillyers and Reynolds, oblivious to the politics and strategies of war, spent most of Sunday morning assessing the impact of bombing on their patients, medical personnel, hospital buildings and sectors. Probationer nurses Grace, Flo, Rose and Gladys were also coming to terms with the night before. Grace, who adopted a matter-of-fact approach to everything in life, simply washed and said her prayers. She had come to nursing from a Girl Guiding background, and had read and inwardly digested every word of *Sick Nursing for Girl Guides* by Gertrude Matheson ARRC. In fact, when it came to the application of linseed and bread poultices, she could give any nursing sister a run for her money. On this particular morning she was tired after working all night, but she still prepared for duty because she was scheduled to work that day. Wearily sorting out a new crisp white apron from her chest of drawers, she climbed into her uniform dress and adjusted her fine, wispy brown hair under a pristine white cap.

Flo, meanwhile, was due to work a set of nights for a week. She had tumbled into bed when the all clear sounded at dawn, and tried in vain to sleep. Briefly thinking that her agitated state of mind could be relieved by some practical activity, she glanced at her knitting needles and deep blue wool on her bedside table. Too tired to follow a knitting pattern, she surveyed her pale blue dress. It was hanging limply on the back of a chair, still stained with Archie's blood. Florence wondered if it was beyond repair. Perhaps she could find a red dye to cover the blood, although she had always favoured blue because it accentuated her eyes. Deciding this was a selfish train of thought when so many had just lost their lives and homes, she eventually got out of bed to make a cup of cocoa, hoping this would induce sleep.

Near the Barking Road, Rose awoke with a dreadful headache in her auntie's bed. She attempted to sit up before deciding this was a colossal mistake. With slightly blurred vision and severe throbbing at her right temple, she reclined back on the feather pillow. At 11 a.m., a neighbour acted as messenger, informing Matron Reynolds that Rose would not be back on duty for at least a couple of days. Her roommate Gladys, usually so composed and self-disciplined, spent most of the morning in Poplar, frantically looking for relatives and friends. After two hours of searching she found her mother and two sisters safe in the cellar of a pub. There were tearful reunions and huge sighs of relief as Gladys assured her mother that their home was still standing. Gladys' mother muttered 'Fank Gaud' over and over under her breath, whilst her daughter offered her own silent prayer of thanks. She could not even begin to contemplate the loss of her mother and sisters so soon after her father's death.

Local officials were also scouring the streets and counting the cost – 1,600 casualties, of which 400 were killed. In addition, 100 tons of shipping had been destroyed along with large industrial factories and warehouses. Writer and broadcaster J.B. Priestley emphatically noted in his postscript of that day: 'We're not really civilians any longer but a mixed bag of soldiers, machine minding soldiers, milkmen and postmen soldiers and housewife and mother soldiers.'[1] Other cities such as Birmingham, Bristol, Coventry and Plymouth were also severely Blitzed, but as Vera Brittain stated: 'London bombed, burned and battered became the symbol of England's anguish, as well as mankind's spiritual failure.'[2]

As Sunday evening approached, the Luftwaffe returned to London, this time killing 412 people and injuring nearly 800. The following night, bombing was again intense, and no longer restricted to the East End. A corner of one of the wards of Great Ormond Street Children's Hospital received a direct hit. An eyewitness described the scene:

In the hospital there was no panic, not even when a high explosive bomb tore a clean hole in the flat roof of the west wing and passed through two upper floors, both reinforced, and detonated on its way through the second of these. The great building shuddered. Four wards and two lift shafts were shattered. Falling glass swept through them like a storm. Fire followed. Within five minutes of this vile attack the hospital's own fire fighters were mastering the flames. Forty six children with their nurses were on the fifth floor. The steel and concrete ceiling above them held firm. There was not a crack in it; not an electric bulb was broken. Confidence of the hospital in its building was justified; the upper floors had taken the worst and the lower floors stood.

With fire above and flood from broken mains in the street behind us and below there was but one thing to do. Safe though the children were for the moment, they must be moved. Then said the nurses calmly smiling to the children in their charge: 'Come along, we're going to see the searchlights.' I thought of Florence Nightingale as the nurses carried the children to the safety of a nearby hospital, while bombs could still be heard exploding and the danger of shell splinters in the air. Some of the children thought it a huge joke to be taken out of bed. It was something different and exciting. All were out safely in ten minutes.[3]

The national press was outraged, and appealed for donations to rebuild the damaged building:

> Just after midnight on September 9th, the Germans dropped a 500lb high explosive on the most famous children's hospital in the world – the Great Ormond Street Hospital – which tore a clean hole through the roof of the west wing, shattering four wards. The damage was great, and falling glass and debris was followed by flames ... The hospital maintains 326 beds and 117 at Tadworth, besides many at convalescent homes. In spite of the war nearly 10,000 little ones were treated in the past year. All donations to this urgent appeal should be addressed to the Chairman, Lord Southwood, at the Hospital for Sick Children, Great Ormond Street, London, W.C.1.[4]

The way in which events unfolded at GOSH was nothing short of a miracle. Staff only managed to evacuate the children safely because an extremely brave ex-Royal Navy stoker named William Pendle managed to draw the fire after the bombing and reduce pressure in the hospital boilers. As he recalled:

> As soon as I went up the stairs to the back of the boiler room I could see what had happened. The bomb had busted the lot, broken the water mains and fired the gas. Seeing what was going on, and the water coming along like a river, I went back to my boiler to draw the fire and get the pressure down. It was lucky I had only one out of three boilers working. It was summer time, and also not working to full strength on account of the war. The pressure being steady at 36lb., I began to rake out the fire and I went on raking until the pressure dropped to nothing.[5]

Against all odds, chest deep in gushing water, surrounded by blazing gas mains, William successfully stopped the boilers from exploding, thus saving the hospital. He was awarded the George Medal for his bravery.

At dawn, an eyewitness surveyed the scene:

I walked through the wards and corridors. The lower ground floor was like a deep river. From the first to the fifth floors all was dark and forlorn. On the sixth there was utter devastation. Battered and twisted cots mingled with shattered telephones, children's toys, story books, fallen masonry and rubble. Still on the pillow of an upturned cot was a baby's cuddly elephant. There had been no children recently in this shattered ward; but a toy cupboard had been burst open, giving an added and authentic horror to the scene. I did not attempt to imagine what that ward might have looked like had the children been in their little cots, instead of in safety down below. As I left this floor I felt something brush against my boot. It was Andy the cat. Andy, alone of all the staff had seen and heard everything on the sixth floor.[6]

At 2.30 a.m., St Thomas' Hospital received a direct hit. A very large bomb crashed down onto Block 1, including Gassiot House, a building which lay between the Treasurer's House and St Thomas' Home. Florence was on night duty taking a well-earned break in the nurses' dining room when the bomb struck without warning. There was no time to take cover. A mighty, deafening roar was accompanied by a forceful suction and compression of air. Lights went out and nurses were knocked to the ground like rows of ninepins. Multiple shards of glass penetrated through their uniforms into their backs. With planes still droning overhead, they could do nothing but lay on the glass-strewn floor, face down on their stomachs, waiting for help to arrive. When Home Sister arrived on the scene with a torch, she immediately issued instructions to night porters to bring surplus mattresses from the stores. Some nurses were able to make their way to the sick bay. Painstakingly, by torchlight, doctors gently removed glass as nurses continued to lie face down on their stomachs. One porter dragging mattresses into the dining room uttered, 'Gor Blimey! So much for sticky tape on windas!' Then came the news that some staff were trapped in the basement of Block 1 and Gassiot House.

Describing the situation at Gassiot House, where two nurses and four massage staff were sleeping, Home Sister recalled:

The bomb had made a direct hit on this spot. Roof and floors had collapsed. Iron girders and wooden beams, a water tank, and a lot of other heavy stuff were piled one on top of another. No light could be thrown on the wreckage because the planes were still overhead. The rescue party did their best. They got into the Treasurer's House and reported that somebody appeared to be still living, though evidently buried under the wreckage, on the third floor of the adjoining house. No attempt could be made to reach this portion of the house from the ground. Something they thought, might be done by breaking through the wall of the Treasurer's House at the third floor. An ill-judged effort might make matters worse. They could only wait, and hope for the dawn.

When it was light I went with the men into the Treasurer's House, the stairs of which could be used. On the third floor I pointed out a fireplace where, if they could cut through, I thought they might find one of our massage staff, Miss Mortimer Thomas. I remembered that she had told me in her belief the corner by the fireplace in her room was the safest part. After this I had to carry on my work elsewhere.[7]

At 7 a.m., rescue workers slowly and carefully began the process of dismantling the wall. They found Australian-born Barbara Mortimer Thomas alive and conscious, but with most of her body trapped under a huge weight of masonry. Medical staff attended the scene to give pain relief and hot drinks to Barbara, and at one point, despite considerable risks, entered her room. Work continued all day long but to no avail. Barbara seemed to recognise that rescue was impossible and urged rescue workers to abandon her and go and help others. Despite all efforts to save her, Barbara lost consciousness and died of severe shock just as an air raid siren signalled the return of the German bombers.

Three other masseuses and two nurses were also crushed to death in this attack. With a heavy heart, Matron Hillyers wrote sympathetic letters of condolence to their distraught families. She knew all of her nurses and medical staff by name, and was acutely aware of their characters and their contribution to St Thomas'. Barbara's loss was particularly hard to bear – a kind, forthright and hard-working lady. Thirty-two-year-old Barbara had been a gifted athlete, and had played hockey for her country before embarking on a massage training course at St Thomas'. In addition to her general medical and surgical work, she was a reforming influence in the maternity field, advocating the widespread use of massage in pregnant women. Only a year before her death, Barbara had co-authored a book entitled *Training for Motherhood* with a colleague in the massage department named Sister Randell. Together they had also been instrumental in establishing widespread prenatal clinics. Writing to her parents, Matron Hillyers described her character: 'She was so gifted and so kind to her patients that her services were always in demand. We can ill spare her. In her short career she had already done much to further the reputation of St Thomas' hospital.'[7]

Despite their obvious distress, family members of the deceased were quick to thank rescue parties who had attempted to free their loved ones. Patients had also been injured at St Thomas' on this dreadful night, but none fatally wounded. Working in her office the next day, ploughing through piles of paperwork and sifting through Ministry of Health circulars, Matron Hillyers came to an unpalatable realisation – London hospitals, previously safe havens for the sick and injured, were no longer untouchable sanctuaries. They had always been on the front line of battles against disease, but now they were on the front line of war.

However, there was not much time for reflecting on events. Casualties flooded through the doors on a nightly basis, all needing urgent attention. Death tolls rose sharply, along with the numbers of critically injured. The recently concussed Rose was preparing to return to work when she found her mother sobbing her heart out at the kitchen table. 'The school,' she sobbed, ''Itler's bombed the school, 'undreds of 'em, 'undreds, ain't nobody left – nobody.' Rose pulled up a chair, placed her hand firmly on top of her mother's and gave it a squeeze. 'I'll make us a cuppa,' she said softly. Her mother was inconsolable. The scale of the tragedy, which occurred on 10 September, was too immense for words.

A parachute bomb had landed on South Halsville School, Agate Street, Canning Town, killing 600 civilians. They had been sheltering for three nights in the school basement waiting for buses to take them out of London. Transport never arrived, and the 600 men, women and children were never seen again. The parachute bomb had wrenched the concrete building, splitting it in two and leaving a crater 20ft deep. Eyewitnesses in the local community heard hundreds of adults and children screaming and crying from beneath the rubble. They were all buried alive. To avoid public panic and a Nazi propaganda victory, government officials claimed that only seventy-seven civilians had died in this incident. East Enders were so enraged by this deception that they stormed the Savoy Hotel, staged a 'sit in' and broke down the doors and locks that had barred their entry to Underground stations. Officials within Chamberlain's government had prevented the use of Underground stations as air raid shelters, ridiculously believing that if Londoners were allowed to take shelter in these stations, they would live a subterranean existence for the entire war! Churchill, however, powerfully asserted that the Underground network obviously provided the best shelters for Londoners, and ordered the removal of all station doors. Henceforth, over 150,000 Londoners took shelter in Underground stations every night. They slept on platforms and escalators. Electricity was turned off at night to allow people to sleep on the rails. Troops also took refuge in Tube stations when they were required to move across London.

A sombre Rose returned to The London to find that several bombs had hit the hospital grounds, but the hospital itself was still intact. After reporting to Matron Reynolds, she walked across to the male surgical ward to check the duty rota. She was delighted to discover that for at least five days she had been given the same duty times as her roommate, Gladys. Sister had thoughtfully placed them together in case Rose needed support. Appreciative of this consideration, Rose walked briskly to the nurses' home to check her laundry. Gladys, meanwhile, was taking a walk along the Embankment, surveying bomb damage. The corner of Westminster Bridge was a wreck and ARP workers were still clearing up rubble from the night before. 'It's a right old mess isn't it?' Gladys turned to see a young woman, adorned in a distinctive St Thomas' cape, staring at the river. 'Yes,' replied Gladys, 'and you lot have copped the worst of it so far.' Flo introduced herself and described the night when she, along with twenty-seven night nurses, was treated for glass wounds. Flo had escaped lightly with only two shards of glass embedded in her right shoulder, whilst others were still suffering from their wounds. The young probationers walked towards the East India docks for a while and promised to meet up at a social gathering organised by the Red Cross on Saturday afternoon. 'Spread the word,' said Flo. 'We're collecting for our pilots.' Gladys nodded and continued her walk alone. Later that evening, as the familiar sound of droning aircraft approached the docks, she told Rose about the Red Cross social and they agreed to go together. Flo walked steadily back to the night nurses' dormitory named Jericho, where she swung her legs onto her freshly made bed, nestled her head into a duck down pillow and slept until 4 p.m. On Friday the 13th, St Thomas' received another direct hit. On this occasion, a large bomb fell on Jericho and a temporary building known as 'E' hut. Luckily only a few staff received minor injuries. A relieved Flo slept in a friend's bedroom whilst surveyors ascertained the safety of Jericho. She awoke Saturday afternoon at 3 p.m., and hurriedly washed and dressed, ready for the fundraising social.

The social was held in a rather rundown church hall, but there were plenty of bustling, cheerful women dishing out cakes and serving tea. Two rather buxom ladies stood at the entrance shaking tins, calling out 'Wings for Victory'. Flo arrived late, at 3.30 p.m. Quickly spotting Gladys and Rose, she made her way over to one of the long wooden trestle tables and helped herself to a tea cake. Declining an offer of parsnip jam and another dubious-looking spread, she sat down beside them. Within minutes they were laughing at shared nursing tales and making jokes about some of the tea ladies, one of whom repeatedly shouted across the room to one of her friends, 'Go on git that down ya old girl.' Time passed very quickly. One of the tea ladies approached them, saying, 'Let's be having ya, that bugger Goering be over soon dropping his little parcels.' As they were leaving, Gladys, who still yearned to be cultured and sophisticated, suggested a trip to see pianist

Myra Hess at one of the National Gallery's lunchtime music concerts. Neither Flo nor Rose knew anything about these concerts, but not wanting to show their ignorance simply nodded in agreement. Rose, almost back to her bubbly self, innocently asked Gladys if it was possible to dance to Myra's music. When Gladys informed her that everyone was required to stay seated throughout the entire performance, she tried to hide her disappointment. They strolled back to The London in silence, both dreading the night ahead.

Whilst Rose, Gladys and Flo had been out socialising, Grace had occupied her time working with a group of Girl Guides. To assist people in the blackout, they had volunteered to paint white lines on the edge of pavements. It was boring but useful work. Grace firmly believed that keeping busy was the only way to deal with war. It was no use at all to sit and worry about things, being busy left no time for worries. Since the bombing of the night nurses' dormitory, Grace had taken to filling up every waking minute of her time. On Sunday, 15 September she was also about to start working alongside Flo on night duty.

Sunday morning began quietly. Then, at 11 a.m., the familiar drone of aircraft could be heard overhead. Yet this time something was different. The noise was louder, more intense. Two hundred and fifty German bombers were approaching London. They were intercepted by the RAF and heated, dramatic dogfights dominated the clear blue skies. Another wave of 250 bombers came across the Channel at 2 p.m. Visiting the headquarters of 11 Group Fighter Command, Churchill confirmed that all RAF squadrons were in the air and fighting, no squadron was held in reserve. Air Marshal Hugh Dowding, head of RAF Fighter Command, had moved planes to the south-east from every area of Britain.

Nurse Monica Baly had a bird's-eye view of the unfolding drama:

It was a golden September day, the sea was blue and calm and I was home on leave from hospital in Bexhill, having obtained the permit which confirmed that Bexhill was my home in what was now a defence zone. Our house was almost on the sea front, which was protected by barbed wire and concrete blocks, and mother was an

A.R.P. warden. Always on the look-out for a supplement to our diet, mother and I decided to take a picnic to Fairlight Glen above Hastings and look for blackberries. We climbed up the deserted path and sat down and surveyed the absolute serenity of the English Channel, never had it looked so beautiful. Then, in the distance we heard the sound of aircraft – ours or theirs? Suddenly the sky was full of activity, we sat transfixed, waves of planes came over, sometimes we could see the markings and there unfolded before our eyes perhaps the greatest battle of the Second World War. There above us were Spitfires and Hurricanes intercepting with bursting gunfire, then one would see a plane on fire spiralling down to the sea. Was this it? Was this the dreaded invasion?

We reckoned we were as safe on the cliff as anywhere but thought we ought to get home as soon as possible as best we could, so, forgetting the blackberries, we clambered back down the path only to find Hastings in confusion. No one was sure what was happening except there was a big battle going on overhead. Now our one thought was to get home to the wireless where the voice of Charles Gardiner in a legendary commentary gave an eye witness account of what had happened and what was happening. Curiously, though one was chilled by the tragedy of burning aircraft which we had seen with our very eyes there was a sense of intense excitement. Later Gardiner was criticised for being carried away with emotion and making the whole thing sound like a football match, but that is how it seemed at the time. What we had witnessed was the pride of the Luftwaffe being picked off by some 300 Spitfires and Hurricanes.[8]

This particular air battle was a defining moment in the Battle of Britain. RAF pilots shot down sixty-one German planes, and lost thirty-one. Formations of Luftwaffe were scattered and they were overwhelmingly defeated. However, this did not stop some of them from returning to drop bombs on London that same evening. Staff at St Thomas' had just finished eating their evening meal when a tirade of bombs came crashing down. The hospital secretary recalled:

Many of us were sitting in the Central Hall talking and reading. I was deep in a novel when the crash came. There was no warning scream of the bomb – only one terrific crack – a blinding flash, and utter darkness. For a time I was conscious only of choking fumes and dust. Rising, I felt for the back of my century old high backed wooden bench. It was not there. I remembered that opposite to me, on similar benches, I had seen our senior physician, resident assistant physician, another doctor, a sister and the house governor. In the darkness and silence of the moment I said to myself: 'They must all be dead.' The next moment voices and movement reassured me. We must have all been stunned slightly from the blast. Lights shined from torches and the air cleared. Flames were now coming from the long corridor, which runs through the hospital north and south from the Central Hall. We had evidently been hit in this vital spot.[9]

Flo and Grace were amongst the nurses and doctors who rushed to help the wounded languishing in the basement, as designated firefighters tackled the blaze. Rescue workers quickly entered the hospital to search for survivors. A wall of flames fuelled by chemicals in the hospital's dispensary dominated the scene. Acids and spirits were all over the floor, burning the boots of dispensers as they scrambled to escape through shattered windows. The outpatient department was flattened, and medical quarters above the basement had collapsed in a heap of rubble. The kitchen, canteen, dispensary and administrative blocks were wrecked. All essential services were out of action. Many of the staff and patients were missing. The Assistant Clerk of the Works sprang into action to help the wounded:

My first job was to assist in moving the canteen wounded to a first aid station under block seven. Turning back to the spot where the bomb had exploded, I searched the main kitchen and found that everyone had escaped by a window. I now heard of missing people, all of whom had been under or near the point at which the bomb entered the hospital. If any were alive, it was pretty plain that they must be under the debris. As I examined the fall, I saw that one very large girder, slipping down from the top floor, was fixed by upright walls at either end, and had caught much of the masonry falling upon it. It appeared to me possible that some of the missing might be found under this girder. I explained the situation as I saw it to the rescue party, suggesting that they tunnel under the girder, which was securely fixed, so far as I could see, and let the debris fall away. They soon got to work. Running considerable risks, they gradually arrived at the place where three of the missing, all severely injured, were lying protected by the girder. These were the Assistant Chaplain (the Rev. Alfred Bird), Mr Nixon, a house physician, and Mr Walker, a dresser. Mr Spilsbury and Mr Campbell were not found until the following day; they had died instantly. Nurse Forbes and Miss Richardson of the first-aid post were found earlier. Both lost their lives through the blast. [10]

Arthur Walker, the dresser who narrowly escaped death on this particular evening, was one of eight medical students sent to St Thomas' for a period of three months to gain trauma and orthopaedic experience. From the age of 12 he had wanted to become a doctor, and was part way through his training when the bomb struck. He remembered very little of that night:

We looked after the patients and when the sirens went we moved everyone to the basement. People were amazingly cheerful, full of guts! I never came across anyone who wanted to give in. In the basement there was a long corridor about three hundred and twenty yards long. Stores were also kept down there. There was lots of piping and concrete. When the bomb hit there were about fifty patients in the basement; eight medical students, doctors, nurses, physiotherapists and anaesthetists. I had just left the operating theatre and that's the last thing I remembered until a week later when I woke up in a sector hospital. I sustained a severe head injury, a fracture to the base of my skull, a scalp wound and superficial burns. I woke up surprised, I had to ask staff what had happened. Then I suffered with post-traumatic stress syndrome and epilepsy.[11]

Arthur remained in a sector hospital for three months and was then sent to recover in a convalescent home for a further three months.

A theatre nurse working with Arthur had clearer memories of that evening:

> An appendix operation was arranged for that night in the emergency theatre in the basement. All was ready when the bomb fell. The theatre sisters, badly shocked and shaken, had to collect their instruments in several inches of water, improvise a new theatre, and re-sterilise on a primus stove. The operation was performed by the light of emergency lamps. This was a ghastly night – no electric light, no gas, about fifty casualties, and many of them very serious. All our available beds were full that night, but by nine o'clock on the Monday morning all the patients were aboard ambulances bound for country hospitals, where we hoped their shattered nerve and bodies would be restored to health. This gave us the empty beds we required for incoming casualties.[12]

In addition to large numbers of casualties, four members of St Thomas' staff died in this attack. Damage inflicted on St Thomas' Hospital buildings amounted to £1.5 million, and dangerous sections were ring-fenced by ropes. Nevertheless, despite the appalling devastation, the following evening the hospital was open for business as usual.

Notes
1 Priestley, J.B., *Postscript London*, 8 September 1940. BBC radio broadcast on the day after the first aerial bombardment.
2 Brittain, V., *England's Hour* (1941), p. 214.
3 Curnock, G.C., *Hospitals Under Fire* (1941), pp. 21–22.
4 *Illustrated London News*, 7 December 1940, p. 33.
5 Curnock, *op. cit.*, pp. 18–19.

6 *Ibid.*, p. 22.

7 London Metropolitan Archives: HO1/ST/A/137/002-139/002 & HO1/ST/A/087/001 & HO1/ST/A/008/018-20.

8 Recollections of Monica Baly, printed in the *Royal College of Nursing History of Nursing Journal*, vol. 3 (1990), pp. 58–59. Monica Baly joined the Princess Mary Royal Air Force Nursing Service. After the war she became a public health nurse and eventually a Royal College of Nursing representative for south-west England. Following her retirement, she studied for a history degree and completed a PhD in history. Dr Monica Baly became a leading light in the field of nursing history and was a personal friend of the author.

9 Curnock, *op. cit.*, p. 45.

10 *Ibid.*, p.48.

11 Walker, Arthur, Oral History Testimony, Imperial War Museum Sound Archive ref:17977/2/1-2.

12 Curnock, G.C., *op. cit.*, p.51.

5

THE RELENTLESS SYMPHONY OF WAR

By mid-September 1940, the battle for air supremacy had reached a climax, and a decisive RAF victory forced Hitler to abandon Operation Sea Lion. Angered and frustrated, he increased the number of bombing raids on major British cities in an attempt to destroy morale. Simultaneously, he redoubled German efforts in the Battle of the Atlantic, hoping to defeat Britain by means of a submarine blockade. However, widespread bombing raids merely strengthened British resolve, and Londoners quickly became used to the regular, relentless symphony of war.

East End buildings bore the deep scars of nightly bombardment just as hospital wards contained the scars of its victims. Yet, compared to the havoc wreaked on St Thomas' during the early September raids, The London Hospital had escaped serious damage. Rose confided to her diary:

Bombs dropping all about us but nothing really serious so far. Our electricity goes off from time to time but we have an emergency generator that kicks in after only a short while. We've also had some very funny incidents. Three of us were in the nurses' swimming pool the other evening when all of a sudden big, burly hospital fire fighters rushed through the doors yelling that they needed our pool water to douse incendiary flames. Mabel, on her seventh lap of breast stroke, was very taken aback by this unexpected turn of events. Our fire fighters explained afterwards that bombs had shattered hospital water pipes. Our swimming pool was the only available water supply until the proper fire brigade turned up. Water shortages also put our hydraulic lifts out of action.

Two nights later, on hearing the siren we were told to go to the basement of Alexandra Luckes nurses' home. Home sister insisted on making a list of our names as we took shelter. She had a job on her hands because there were at least a hundred and fifty of us all told. We squeezed in tightly together and sang songs to drown out the racket of bombs. Lots of renditions of old favourites and of course Run Rabbit Run. Home sister started singing Somewhere over the Rainbow then she forgot the words. We were all laughing loudly. Then we got a direct hit. Sounds of laughter died down, everything was dark. Walls started to crumble and the ground vibrated underneath, but sister said it was safer for us to stay put. Waiting for the all clear seemed to take forever. For a while I was worried about Gladys, she went deadly quiet. I thought she'd been injured. Turned out she was upset because she'd broken a thermometer the day before and money to buy another one is going to be docked out of her wages.

At any rate we survived the night – all of us thankful to be squinting our eyes at morning sunlight. Much damage done to nurses' home.

Nurses were housed in makeshift accommodation until walls were made safe and electrical supplies restored. Then, on 17 September, The London felt the full force of the enemy when a landmine attached to a parachute landed with a tremendous crash in the hospital grounds. Subsequently, after three days, another bomb became wedged between the recently opened Department of Medicine and the Outpatient Department. Acting Matron Miss Burgess was knocked off her feet by the forceful blast, thrown to the floor and cut by shards of glass.

Delayed action bombs were found in the hospital grounds and in the outpatient clinics. All of these were eventually rendered safe by the bomb disposal team.

On 24 September, the king and queen embarked on a morale-boosting tour of the East End. The London was celebrating its 200th anniversary. An observer on the hospital wards noted:

> The patients were delighted to see the kindly, simple way the King and Queen moved from bed to bed. One aged Londoner, who was thought to be asleep, called to the Queen: 'Where's your old man?' The King, hearing, went back with a smile and a greeting. One patient was contemptuous of 'Jerrys' efforts.' 'When you've had a packet like mine and got through with it you don't worry anymore. Will you write it down mister? And don't forget it, if there are any George medals going about they should be given to the nurses. I've seen them going up and down this very ward more than once when the bombs are falling, and not paying any attention to them, only talking to the patients and telling them not to worry. Yes, and I've seen a surgeon putting stitches into a fireman's nose in that bed over there, the night a bomb fell in the garden; just as cool as if nothing was happening.'[1]

Dr Archibald Clark-Kennedy, a physician at The London, also noted that the royal visit began with an 'all clear' but ended with a full-scale alert:

> That same evening after a rather better dinner than usual, there came a startling whizz – but no explosion. We went out to investigate. A gaping hole had appeared in the garden where the statue of Queen Alexandra stands, caused presumably by a delayed action bomb that might go off at any moment. Wards at risk were cleared as far away and as quickly as possible. But we had to wait six whole days – while this menace persisted – before Lieutenant Davies, who had defused the bomb that threatened St Paul's came down with his team to deal with it. Our bomb, for some technical reason, could not be defused. It had to be covered up with tons of earth and detonated. These

tons went up in the air. No windows had been broken, but tattered sandbags, caught up in the telephone wires crossing the garden, persisted drearily for weeks.[2]

Medical and nursing staff shrugged off this latest bomb in their usual dismissive manner. Scurrying down the women's medical ward carrying a bedpan, Rose cheerfully quipped to one of her patients: 'Don't worry, it's just a little birthday present from Goering!' Gladys meanwhile adopted a protective motherly approach to her patients, chivvying them along with gentle reassurances as though they were helpless, frightened children. Gladys had assumed the role of mother from early childhood, her character fashioned by years of tending to her invalid father and younger siblings whilst her mother took in washing to make ends meet. She had taken to nursing like a duck to water, accustomed as she was to putting the needs of others first. Popular with staff and patients alike, Gladys glided effortlessly through the wards. Taller than her peers, slim with glossy, liquorice-coloured hair and deep blue eyes, she somehow managed to walk elegantly in spite of clumpy standard-issue shoes. When tirades of deafening bombs came crashing down she gave no hint of panic, instilling in her patients a sense of well-being and security. Whereas Rose used humour and wit as a defence mechanism, Gladys favoured determined stoical endurance. She would never admit to the severe thud inside her head as terrifying explosions caused violent tremors beneath her feet, nor to the palpitations which accompanied each wailing warning siren. Concerned only for her patients and colleagues, she successfully supressed all fear.

Structured drills and procedures also helped to calm staff nerves as Dr Clark-Kennedy asserted:

There was no panic in Whitechapel. In the hospital everybody soon settled down to their routine. After dinner in the basement the staff picked up their tin hats and proceeded to their allotted posts: the house governor and secretary to their offices, whence one of them always toured the wards when a raid was on: the surveyor to his control centre and his men to their observation stations to report where bombs fell or incendiaries landed; the doctors to the receiving room, resuscitation room and theatres.[3]

By this stage, The London had acquired a healthy annual financial surplus of £40,000 and was renting a hutted hospital in Brentwood. This institution included all main branches of medicine and surgery, and ensured that patients were directly cared for by The London medical and nursing staff. Consultants also benefited from this acquisition, since they were able to dispense with sector hospitals for teaching purposes and transfer medical students to an allotted annexe.

In addition to acquiring hutted buildings to supplement patient bed capacity, hospital matrons were attempting to find extra accommodation for cleaning staff and ward maids, many of whom were being made homeless on a nightly basis. Ruth Clarkson, Matron of Royal Waterloo Hospital, writing to the House Committee, outlined her staffing problems:

> The domestic difficulties are great. Since the beginning of the air raids we have only had 4 daily workers available instead of 7. The shortage of maids is also acute. At the moment we have only 4, though the return of 2 who are on holiday is hoped for. The nurses in the preliminary training school have been splendid during the last month in helping domestically, as have all members of the nursing staff, but it is a most grave and unsatisfactory state of affairs for which I have so far been able to find a remedy.
>
> Miss Ryman, who works in the linen room, was away last week. When she returned yesterday she found her home in ruins. She hopes that a good part of her possessions may be salvaged, and she is already setting about establishing herself elsewhere. Meantime she is housed here as she had nowhere to go, and for this she is extremely grateful. By her absence last week she forfeited her week's salary (£1-8/-), and she has offered to forego a portion of this week in return for the consideration shown her. Miss Ryman is a very loyal, devoted and

valuable member of the staff, and I would recommend that she should be given her full salary. She often works longer than she is required to do, and all she does is well done.[4]

On 27 September, it was the turn of St Thomas' Hospital to receive a royal visit. Both king and queen spent over two hours viewing structural bomb damage and talking to staff and patients. On the same day, Londoners elsewhere were treated to the unusual spectacle of a zebra trotting along recently swept pavements, making its way to Camden Town. A bomb had landed on London Zoo and he was one of several animals temporarily on the loose.

Back on day duty at St Thomas', Flo and Grace were hard at work on a male surgical ward. Each bright and airy ward contained thirty beds. Day shifts began at 7 a.m. and finished at 8 p.m. Once sister had said ward prayers and given a report on each patient, breakfasts were served and then cleared away. Morning tasks included the collection of sputum trays, cleaning and tidying bedside lockers, and helping patients with bed baths and ordinary baths. In addition, there were patients to get ready for operations, wound dressings to prepare and instruments to sterilise. Patients in a critical condition were deemed as special cases and cared for by a designated nurse on a one-to-one basis. Male surgical was one of St Thomas' busiest wards, teeming with activity. Surgical cases ranged from routine ingrowing toenail removals and hernia repairs, to emergency admissions such as those suffering from a burst appendix, bowel obstructions or stomach ulcers. When bombing raids were severe, surgical wards often contained an overflow of casualties – either because they were medically unfit to travel to sector hospitals, or because there were insufficient ambulances to transport the sheer volume of injured. Grace wrote to one of her four older brothers:

Days are never dull. Emergencies come in at all hours and I see each one as an opportunity to learn. A man arrived yesterday with dreadful abdominal crush injuries, caused by a collapsed car jack. He was in theatre ages – nobody really expected him to pull through. Shallow breathing, skin cold, clammy, completely without colour. I could hardly find his pulse … at 2pm sister thought he'd died, yet miraculously he is still in the land of the living today. His wife is a forlorn figure who sits huddled by his bedside, skinny, wretched looking with eyes blotched and swollen from sobbing.

Loads of air raid victims were admitted overnight, most suffering from burns or blast injuries. Nearly all of them got patched up and dispatched to sectors. Only a few still lingering here. Other cases are quite straightforward at the moment, though a gall bladder patient in bed seven is infuriatingly nosy. He keeps asking me if someone's died every time we put screens round a bed! Sister is a martinet but her ward runs like clockwork. Work is tiring and sometimes exasperating but we are getting used to Jerry's frequent visits. It is surprising how quickly the extraordinary becomes ordinary.

Everyone gets along very well. In our nurses' home, before the air raid siren goes, we off-duty nurses perch ourselves around the solitary gas fire toasting bread on the end of long handled forks. This is when we swap sad or funny stories about our patients. In the dining room we are not allowed to talk shop so 'toasting time' is the only chance we get to confide in each other. Home sister once made a feeble attempt to break up this treasured interval by trying to convince us that bread has more goodness in it before it is toasted – but of course none of us believed her.

As a third-year probationer, Grace was required to maintain certain nursing equipment and assist patients at mealtimes. She was allowed to do simple dressings and take clinical observations such as patients' temperatures, pulse rates and, if no doctors were about, blood pressure recordings. Whereas Flo, a mere second-year, was still confined to boringly mundane cleaning and preparation work. She was also expected to help with domestic work because of a shortage of ward maids. Flo confessed in her diary:

I don't mind cleaning up blood or vomit but collecting and washing sputum trays makes my stomach heave. Why do men spit so much? You can tell the heavy woodbine smokers, they cough up yellowy, green or brown gooey muck. It's enough to make anyone feel sick. Then we have to label trays in case doctor wants to examine them on his rounds, so they are left congealing for hours before we can clean up. Enamel dishes are so hard to get clean. We have to use a horrible caustic solution, which makes my eyes run and stings my nose. I can smell it for ages afterwards.

Getting dressings done is boring but not so bad. They send us huge rolls of gauze which we have to cut to size then pack very tightly in big round drums. Once we've finished a porter takes them away for autoclaving. Instruments are sterilised by boiling them in water. Staff nurse usually does this job in case we probationers get the timing wrong. We get treated as though we are complete idiots.

A long letter from Archie arrived today. He says he is receiving the very best of care but none of his nurses are a patch on me. It seems he will be out of action for at least six weeks. We will certainly remember our first date. He is so very handsome and I miss his cheeky dimpled smile. It was terribly brave of him to protect me. I must knit him a pair of khaki socks as a thank you as soon as I am able, or perhaps a pullover. He's saving his money to buy me a new dress, so I must tell him that I managed to turn my old one into a perfectly serviceable blouse. It goes exceptionally well with my grey skirt. I'm also making a winter dress from some ancient brocade curtains. Once I cut away the faded bits nobody will be able to tell the difference. I may even have enough left over for a matching hat.

In her off-duty hours, Flo spent much of her time embroidering a tablecloth and other items for her bottom drawer, and knitting socks and balaclavas for the RAF and the firemen. Two addresses lay neatly by her bedside. The first was: 'The RAF Comforts Committee, 20, Berkeley Square, London W1'. And the other was: 'Mrs Thomas Hutchinson, Auxilliary Fire Service, War Comforts Department, 43, Green Street, Park Lane London W1'.

With a sense of fairness in all things, Flo divided the fruits of her needlework between both addresses equally. Before the war she had managed to accrue a reasonable stock of wool and threads, but these were now diminishing at an alarming rate. There was a particular shortage of embroidery threads and her mother had been unravelling dyed dishcloths in an effort to replenish her stocks.

Across the corridor in the nurses' home, Grace, who loved her food, devoted her free time to discovering new recipes and diligently teaching telegraphic communications skills to Girl Guides. Currently working her way through a book entitled *Fifty Ways to Cook with Tripe*, she assured Flo that tripe was just the thing for making sick people well. Flo remained unconvinced, but with a mother in the local Women's Institute and a father working as an ARP warden, Grace was imbued with a sense of community spirit and cookery prowess which bordered on religious zeal.

Over at The London, introverted Gladys preferred to use her off-duty time to listen to classical music or visit family, whereas the irrepressible Rose usually headed off to see the latest cinema film, or to meet up with friends to go dancing. As much as possible, probationer and trained nurses living in London attempted to live normal lives, amongst the ever-growing mountains of rubble. The familiar nightly drone of German bombers, however, precluded many activities. Some hospital workers were not even able to get home at night. As a physician at The London recalled:

In the middle of dinner, a succession of whizzes and bangs swept across from the direction of Aldgate. All dived under the tables for cover again (I can remember hitting my head hard against that of the professor of medicine in the melee). The college had been hit; that was clear almost at once, and its sole occupant, my lame secretary (to whom I had given permission to sleep there during the week as she had difficulty in getting home at night) emerged shaken but unhurt from the basement. A bomb had fallen through the roof, exploded on the concrete floor of the dissecting room – empty of even dead bodies – and blown the bacteriology room to pieces.[5]

Fortunately, the hospital's considerable supply of radium had been relocated and buried in a big pit in Bedfordshire prior to the Blitz. Other London hospitals had made similar arrangements for the storage of radium. Blissfully unaware of invisible chemical dangers, newspapers focussed on the need to raise money to repair visible damage:

Resident in Westminster we have often leaned over the Victoria Gardens to watch 'Old Man River' pass to and fro in his sombre fashion, and realised that on the south bank our most beautiful hospital, St Thomas', was, indeed, a worthy national possession. To learn that it has suffered from destructive enemy bombs has aroused a deep sense of indignation. 'It will never be rebuilt,' we heard one fatuous person remark recently. Of course it will be rebuilt and right soon we hope. An appeal is to be made at an early date for the upkeep of our voluntary hospitals; and should an appeal for St Thomas' hospital be made direct to the 100,000 nurses on the State Register, in the name of Florence Nightingale whose pioneer school of nursing is attached to it, they should be able to rouse a vast amount of interest in a rebuilding scheme which might spread far and near.

Again, the splendid London Hospital, which has been badly damaged – the hospital of the East End poor – also victimised by the barbarous Hun, should add the magnetic name of the 'Prince of Beggars,' the late revered Lord Knutsford, to any special appeal in its support. There is little doubt that our people will make it a work of honour, when time permits, to restore and improve every atom of damage done by enemy bombs throughout the country. The valuable lives lost cannot be restored – doctors, nurses, patients – but they can be held in honoured memory and be associated with the scenes of their martyrdom.[6]

As the number of Londoners heading for shelter in Underground stations increased, female ARP workers were encouraged to attend courses on how to deliver babies. This was a dangerous and worrying trend. The Board of Midwifery responded assertively:

The Board was informed that in certain parts of the country women in the A.R.P. service were being given a short, superficial training in midwifery (including a method of expressing the placenta). While the Board fully appreciated the laudable motive behind the giving of such training, it felt bound to draw attention to the dangers likely to arise in view of the unsatisfactory and incomplete nature of the instruction. It informed the Ministry of Health of its views and suggested that, if a woman begins labour in an air raid shelter during an air raid, she should be regarded as a civilian casualty and conveyed to a hospital or first aid post where a doctor is in attendance, or, if there is not time or the opportunity, a doctor or midwife should be summoned. Reference was also made to the kind attention which the Board considered could be given to unqualified persons without endangering the safety of mother and child. The Ministry of Health agrees to take steps to prevent A.R.P. midwifery instruction and issue guidance leaflets to instruct that doctor or midwife should be summoned as soon as possible.[7]

Registered nurses were also staunchly defending their profession. Miss N. Dunkley SRN, Chairman of the Guild of Nurses, wrote to the Talks Director of the BBC after listening to a talk in the series *Calling all Women*:

Dear Sir,

At the end of the one o' clock news today a letter was read about the hospital services in London in which nurses received the highest praise, only to be followed by a talk, one sentence of which did almost irreparable harm to the same profession.

In the 'Calling all Women' series, the speaker today mentioned that women in a certain village had themselves added to the equipment of a first aid post, fitting it and also using it as an out-patient department, then saying, 'They are now as capable as any trained nurses to deal with casualties.'

It seems that nurses are always 'obeying the country's call' are never to get their deserts. May I suggest that you approach the National Council of Nurses, 19, Queen's Gate, S.W.7., to which more than 50 associations of trained nurses are affiliated, asking them to provide a speaker and talk on 'The Importance of the Trained Nurse to the Country.'

Last week 122 hospitals were advertising for young women to commence training as nurses. After hearing the talk this afternoon girls will think it is no use training, and the sick of the country will eventually suffer.

Kindly forward the enclosed letter to the speaker, Mrs Tate, M.P.

Yours faithfully

Nellie Dunkley, S.R.N. M.B.C.N. Chairman[8]

Nellie had included a separate letter addressed to Miss Mavis Tate, Conservative MP for Frome, chiding her for her serious and most misleading statement. Though Nellie also acknowledged that since Miss Tate had previously stood up for registered nurses in parliament by opposing the official recognition of assistant nurses, her offending statement in *Calling all Women* was probably an accidental error of judgement. Nellie's letter to the MP was reasonably conciliatory, therefore:

> I feel sure you would not deliberately disparage our profession, and as a closer knowledge of our training would have enabled you to avoid such a catastrophe, shall have much pleasure in arranging a visit to one of our training schools if you will give me some alternative dates.[9]

Both nursing and midwifery problems, however, emanated from the Ministry of Health. Indeed, ministers in this department were of the opinion that nursing was merely an extension of motherhood. As far as they were concerned, nurses simply gave out bedpans and mopped the occasional fevered brow. There was no recognition of nursing expertise. Thus, academic qualifications for entrance to nurse training were scrapped, and a roll for assistant nurses established. Cadet schemes were also introduced, whereby girls as young as 15 were able to enter the profession. By this stage, hospitals across the country were suffering from a loss of senior nurses, caused primarily by the unrestricted flow of registered nurses into the armed forces. This was compounded by a disjointed CNR and shortages in the midwifery, psychiatric and sanatorium sectors of nursing. Not surprisingly, the health of the civilian population began to suffer.

Notes

1 Curnock, G.C., *Hospitals Under Fire* (1941), pp. 33–34.
2 Clark-Kennedy A.E., *London Pride: the Story of a Voluntary Hospital* (1979), p. 218. Lieutenant Robert Davies of the Royal Engineers was awarded the George Cross for his bravery in dealing with a bomb that threatened to destroy St Paul's Cathedral. The bomb was dropped by the Luftwaffe on the night of 8–9 September and had lodged so deep in the ground that it took three days to extricate. Lieutenant Davies drove the bomb away from the cathedral and disposed of it on Hackney Marshes.
3 *Ibid.*, p. 218.
4 London Metropolitan Archives: Matron's Report Book, Royal Waterloo Hospital: 24 September 1940 reference: H01/RW/C/01/003.
5 Clark-Kennedy, A.E., *op. cit.*, p. 219.
6 Editorial, *British Journal of Nursing*, October 1940.
7 *British Journal of Nursing*, October 1940, p. 179.
8 Dunkley, N., letter to Talks Director BBC, dated 24 October 1940.
9 Dunkley, N., letter to Miss Mavis Tate MP, sent c/o BBC dated 24 October 1940.

6

DANGER IN SAFETY

The pivotal Battle of Britain drew to a close at the end of September. The German Luftwaffe had lost 1,408 aircraft, compared with the RAF's loss of 697 aircraft. Operation Sea Lion was postponed indefinitely. In October, a seriously thwarted Hitler met up with his bombastic ally Mussolini at Brenner Pass, to discuss war strategies. Daylight raids over London began to peter out, but night bombing continued apace. As dusk fell, Londoners routinely trekked to private and public shelters. However, a lack of medical provision for those sheltering in seventy-nine Underground stations was causing concern. An article written by a special correspondent entitled 'Danger in Safety' explained the problem:

> Although the government has accepted the use of underground stations as air raid shelters, it has done nothing to protect the health of the thousands of those who seek shelter. There are no A.R.P. wardens or first aid services, and lavatory accommodation is totally inadequate. Mothers who go down to the platform for the night are so grateful their children are in safety from the bombs that they are risking the greater danger of epidemic.

A woman who has been one of those people sharing nightly refuge in our London stations said yesterday, 'Last night I was getting my bag ready on the station platform when an elderly gentleman nearby suddenly collapsed. In any other shelter he would have been attended to immediately by trained men or women. But what happened here was that he was surrounded by a crowd of hysterical women who did nothing for him. I managed to get through them and loosened his collar. I had some eau de cologne with me and I used this to bring him round. He had only fainted but he might easily have been in a more serious condition – and it was hopeless to find a first aid worker. I went to get him some water and was told by railway officials that water taps were not turned on until 9pm.

He eventually got to the lift shaft where there was more air, but had to put up with children clambering over him as they played.[1]

Initial difficulties associated with the organisation of night-time shelters were centred on spheres of influence. London police were prevented from marshalling crowds of people on Underground stations because they were outside their jurisdiction. Members of London Passenger Transport Board were inundated with requests for makeshift toilets, adequate drinking water, hot drinks and food. Furthermore, newspaper reports persisted in highlighting the lack of Underground facilities and argued that the situation was seriously affecting morale. According to the Home Intelligence Service, morale relied on the provision of a safe haven, hot food and a good night's sleep. Yet government departments and council officials dragged their feet over the provision of basic medical care, security and comfort for nightly trekkers. It was left to the voluntary organisations of the Order of St John of Jerusalem and the British Red Cross to bring a sense of reassuring order to existing chaos. These voluntary bodies – who were already training VAD nurses for civilian and military purposes, and running and staffing a system of auxiliary hospitals and first aid posts – extended their remit to care for those sheltering underground. Henceforth, all stations included first aiders, hot food and drinks, toilet facilities, blankets, children's toys, books and entertainment.

Embracing the concept of an Underground community, those seeking shelter began to chalk out their sleeping areas on station platforms and share their meagre food rations with others. Coat hooks were drilled into station walls to hold overcoats, dressing gowns and hats. Children commandeered any available space, chalk, stones and twigs to play hopscotch, pick-up sticks, and noughts and crosses. They played conkers and memory games, and sat in circles to sing songs and eat meals. Londoners developed a nightly subculture, exchanging snippets of news, telling jokes and pouring scorn onto the enemy. Tightly packed onto platforms like sardines in a can, babies were born and children scampered around as gossiping women, dressed in pinafores or house coats, knitted pullovers and darned socks. Bored men in flat caps and rolled up shirt sleeves dangled small babies on their laps, polished their boots, played darts or cards, read newspapers or played accordions, banjos or flutes to pass the time. Each family brought quilted or rough wool blankets, food and water. In battered suitcases or parcels tied with newspaper and string, they also brought with them a few family clothes and treasured photographs. Nobody could predict what each night would bring, or whose house would be still standing in the morning. Only one thing was certain: the fact that camaraderie forged during intense night-time raids spilled over into daylight hours.

Travelling in the autumn sunshine on her way to inspect sector hospitals, Matron Hillyers was reading her newspaper out loud to her amiable driver, Thomas. She liked to keep abreast of current affairs and her frequent trips to the countryside in the back of a comfortable old Austin afforded her this opportunity. Shaking her head in disbelief at some of the stories, she voiced her incredulity at an article which claimed that psychiatrists in London had not seen any evidence of nerves or shell shock in the London population. Matron was indignant, 'They would jolly well see some if they moved their clinics to Guildford or Woking!' Matron was convinced that once severe air raid casualties were transported from London to sectors, they were, in essence, out of sight and out of mind. Thomas nodded sagely in agreement. Press reports which claimed that nobody ever panicked under the relentless ear-splitting din of thundering bombs were also dismissed with a wave of Matron's hand. She knew from recent experience that whilst the majority of Londoners remained calm and determined through the raids, there were also those who lost control of their emotions. Hysterical screaming, uncontrollable shaking, gibberish talk and catatonic expressions could all be found in nightly triage rooms, whereas the seriously injured were in shock, deathly pale with glazed expressions, quiet, rigidly still, with deep pain etched across their faces. Folding her newspaper and placing it neatly beside her on the empty back seat, Matron Hillyers gave a huge sigh. Newspaper reports were heavily censored, and it was becoming increasingly difficult to discern news from propaganda. Despite this, articles published in the *New York Times* repeatedly cited London newspapers as 'Heroes of the Press', claiming:

> London newspapers of these terrible days are in themselves documents that deserve to be treasured. They prove better than speeches of cabled dispatches or photographs that life in the great city goes on in spite of Hitler's efforts to strangle it. The London milkman goes his rounds; subway trains and buses keep moving in spite of all obstacles, light and power services are maintained as far as possible and newspapers appear as usual. Thousands of homely men and women who maintain the essential services of London are helping fully as much as fighter squadrons and anti-aircraft gunners to keep the body and soul of London alive. Whatever the risks they face them without flinching.[2]

Matron, having given up on her newspaper in disgust, wound down the car window to breathe the fresh country air and view the stunning autumn scenery. Gazing out of the car, she could see majestic trees of gold, red and amber lining the horizon and dotting the hedgerows. There were rolling fields of muted shades of green, divided by brooks, rivers and canals. Norman churches nestled amid woodlands and sunshine rippled through leafy lanes. Surrounded by such glorious scenery, it was hard to believe the country was at war. Turning her attention back to work, she scanned her schedule. Top of her list of patients to visit that day was Dr Arthur Walker, who had sustained a fracture to the base of his

skull at St Thomas' during the dreadful 15 September bombing. He was
one of many patients who had experienced shell shock as a result. He
had also experienced episodes of epilepsy and was likely to be in hospital
until Christmas.[3]

In her role as Superintendent of St Thomas' nurse training school,
Matron also wanted to catch up with her sector hospital probationers
to assess their progress. There were worrying trends in nurse training,
and one in three probationers were dropping out of training before the
end of their first year. This situation was not helped by the government's
decision to flood hospitals with young girls who didn't know their
fibroids from their fistulas. Senior nurse tutors were in despair at this
official emphasis on the quantity of nurse probationers, rather than the
quality. Neither were they impressed by the Alien Act, since alien nurses
made up 10 per cent of all nurses in training.

Matron Hillyers acknowledged that nurses were undoubtedly
working under stress, and there was considerable evidence to suggest
that civilian nursing services were on the brink of collapse. She laid her
schedule to one side and picked up her nursing journal to read the list
of disciplinary cases, frowning with concern at the number of registered
nurses having been placed before the General Nursing Council (GNC)
that summer; one of whom she knew very well:

Miss Edna Ruth Poole, S.R.N., 67433 was charged at Birmingham
City Police Court on July 30th 1940, with stealing 100 tablets of
morphia from the Aero factory, where she was engaged as a nurse. She
pleaded overwork and an attack of influenza, and took the tablets for
the purpose of committing suicide. After leaving the works, she put
all the tablets down a drain in the road, and had taken none of them.
The Council considered the case *in camera*, and, although regarding
the offence as a very serious matter, postponed judgement for a term
of six months, Miss Poole to place herself under the care of a medical
practitioner, and to send in a report at the end of that period.

Miss Mary Elizabeth Thompson, S.R.N., 50234, a member of the
Private Nursing Staff of St Thomas' Hospital, London, was charged at

the South Western Police Court on August 16th 1940, with obtaining heroin by forged prescriptions on 24 occasions, and discharged under the Probation of Offenders Act. The matron at the hospital and the superintendent of the Private Staff, the latter who attended with Miss Thompson, bore witness to her previous very good conduct and said they would have no hesitation in taking her back on the staff. The Council considered the case *in camera*, and while not minimizing these crimes – forgery and taking drugs – both serious offences, had agreed to postpone judgement for a period of one year, Miss Thompson to remain under medical supervision and to keep the Registrar aware of her movements.[4]

The list continued, and the number of disciplinary cases involving registered nurses grew steadily. These were first heard at local police courts, then placed before the GNC for consideration a few months later. Most involved drug misuse and the nurses charged were usually repentant. More serious cases were those involving patients. Matron Ruth Clarkson included one such case in her report to the Board of Governors:

Gentlemen,

    I submitted to the medical committee a report on Nurse Miriam Grey. She recently gave to a patient an overdose of a sedation, and in doing so broke all the rules laid down by this hospital in accordance with the Dangerous Drugs Act requirements. The patient suffered no ill. Nurse agrees that she was at fault, but her attitude when censored was flippant and lacking in any sense of responsibility. Nurse Grey is not in any way typical of a Royal Waterloo Hospital nurse, and I feel strongly that she is not entitled to the hospital certificate or badge. She has completed her full period of training and I do not think that it is possible to prevent her entry for the State Examination.[5]

Instances which placed the patient in danger were, in fact, commonplace. Moreover, there was little a matron could do except appeal to hospital governors or the GNC to take action. Since staff shortages were worsening by the day, both these bodies were reluctant to dispense with the services of any nurse, except in the most severe of circumstances. Indeed, London nurses who remained in the city were being called upon to help with outpatient clinics in areas where hospitals had relocated. Matron Clarkson, returning from a well-deserved vacation, found a request for registered nurses waiting on her desk:

> During my absence on leave a request came through the Sector Matron, from All Saints Hospital Southwark, asking if we can help in any way with their out-patient clinic. The hospital itself is transferred to Woking, and their own sister has been coming up weekly from there to do the work. During the winter months this arrangement is not practicable. Last Wednesday I made financial arrangements for Sister Jennings to go. She conducted one small clinic in the morning and one in the afternoon, which involved her absence from 9.30am till 4pm. She was provided with lunch at the hospital and her travelling expenses amounted to three pence. I sent a senior nurse with sister so that, in the event of it being inconvenient to spare sister from here, nurse could undertake the work.[6]

Matron Hillyers, in her triple role as matron of St Thomas' Hospital, superintendent of its nursing school and sector matron, had dealt with this request for nurses and a myriad of others. Furthermore, given the shortages of nursing staff, it was not surprising for skill levels to be interchangeable. Long hours, poor pay, petty restrictions and rigid lifestyle were competing with war-related jobs, which required shorter hours, were better paid and offered more freedom. Munitions factories were particularly popular with young girls. Over 20 per cent of girls who had applied to be probationer nurses before the war had written to their nursing schools to inform them that they still intended to do nurse training at some stage, but preferred to wait until the war was over. There were also difficulties associated with hiring residential cleaning staff, as Matron Clarkson noted:

The steps taken to supplement the resident staff are:

a)   Application to all the usual sources in the north of England and elsewhere.

b)   Application to Registers.

c)   Application to Labour Exchange – both adult and juvenile.

None of these have been successful, but the necessary work is being quite satisfactorily done by daily workers.[7]

Residential work of all kinds was becoming less popular with women, especially in London, where women were often required to take care of bombed-out family members. Nursing shortages were most acute in isolated areas such as mental asylums and sanatoriums. Psychiatric nursing had long been a male domain because physical strength was often required to restrain patients. This field of nursing was seriously depleted by the number of men who had joined the armed forces. Sanatorium nursing was the least popular of all nursing fields, not only because such institutions were in extremely isolated areas, but also because many nurses actually caught tuberculosis from their patients and died as a result.

Even young probationers in general hospitals, who were prepared to put up with poor pay, did not always take to nursing. Rose had encouraged her 18-year-old cousin to become a probationer, but the latter was so appalled by the work she only stayed in training for three weeks. She tearfully confessed to Rose and her friends:

I didn't think I was going to get killed. But after a few weeks in hospital, nursing, I was so horrified at the work, and having been in the sixth form at school and then having to do bedpans and spittoons, I thought I might as well get killed then I would be a heroine, you know, I really did think like that – I hated it so much, but I was too proud to go home. So I thought that if I did get killed then I would be out of it and they would all be crying round my graveside. That's really true – I did feel that. The next job I was given was to go and help lay someone out. I had never seen a dead person, and they cut the nails of people when they lay them out in hospital. I don't know if they do at home. And the nurse was cutting the nails and there was a little blood oozing. I said 'Gosh that's going to hurt when he wakes up' and she said, 'When do you think that's going to be – up with St Peter, because he's dead you fool.'[8]

Rose, who also dreaded collecting early morning spittoons, was sympathetic. Nursing was not an easy job, and certainly not for the faint-hearted. She comforted her cousin with endless cups of milky cocoa and suggested gently that perhaps she was more suited to communications work. Sitting round the gas fire at toasting time, other nurses voiced their complaints. A staff nurse named Molly recalled her training:

We had mauve and white checks for the students in training with big puffed sleeves, and then long white sleeves which were detached. These white detachable sleeves had to be removed when you did anything that required you to roll up your sleeves in the ordinary way. But if you were giving meals or medicines you had to put your sleeves on, and if you talked to sister you had to put your sleeves on. If you had to bring her a message you had to quickly stop and put your sleeves on. We grumbled about her – we were only young girls – looking back I can see she was very fair, but if there was any sliding of discipline then you were really for it. I had one day off a month, and quite often was told the day before when the day off was to be, and certainly for our off-duty we were told in the morning. We went on at 7am and had to get everything spick and span for sister at 8.30. She said ward prayers and afterwards we all lined up and she said 'Now you can be off this morning nurse, and you can be off this afternoon.' So you rushed to see if your friends had the same luck or misfortune. The matron used to do her round every morning, and she wore white gloves, and she would go round and inspect all the sluices because we were responsible for the sluices and bathrooms. You were hauled up before her if she found anything untoward that you were responsible for because we all had our own jobs.[9]

Rose was just thinking that not an awful lot had changed from staff nurses' day when the siren rang out again. Toasting time was over. Although not officially on duty, all nurses donned their uniforms and hurried to the wards to see if their services were needed. On this particular evening, all patients were already in the basement when Rose arrived. Cheered by the banter and chatter of patients, she moved across the wards to help a junior nurse give out hot drinks. The familiar drone of planes signalled yet another night of terror but Rose was feeling relaxed. She was looking forward to a day off the following day, so she would try and sleep in the early hours. As her friend Gladys was fond of telling her, everyone nowadays was surviving on five hours' sleep a night. Patients, often assisted by sedatives, slept better than most. Thundering ground-shaking dins, interspersed with the *ack-ack* rhythm of anti-aircraft fire, provided a nightly symphony of sound that patients began to ignore. Furthermore, doctors like Dr Clark-Kennedy were commenting on the fact that other than bomb victims, the health of Londoners was better than expected:

> The winter is now on us and the number of beds in action in the hospital [The London] for ordinary cases has been increased to three hundred and fifty to meet the higher rate of sickness. The blitz is not associated with any increase in it. Rather, the reverse seems to be the case, the population of London healthier than before to a degree difficult to account for in terms of orthodox medicine. Shelter life breeds its diseases; gravitational oedema, bed sores, pressure palsies. But there is no increase in respiratory and gastro-intestinal infection as has been feared. Indeed, it is difficult not to include that the community spirit and that of mutual help engendered by hatred of a common enemy, and determination to stick it out, has raised resistance to disease above its average level.[10]

Measuring the nation's overall health in wartime, however, was problematic in many respects, particularly since the healthiest members of the population were away fighting in the armed forces. Poor record-keeping and the tidal waves of evacuees moving to and fro between the cities and the countryside also obscured, and in some instances distorted, the general picture of health. Government ministers had expected child health to deteriorate because of war conditions and had done their best to mitigate this possibility. Epidemics of typhoid and other waterborne illnesses were expected to take hold as a result of bombed water pipes, and diseases associated with malnutrition were predicted. Yet, notwithstanding the dubious record-keeping in some quarters, it was clear that children and adults were in much better general health than anticipated. However, in terms of childhood epidemics, the picture was far from rosy.

Prevalent epidemics during the Blitz included: diphtheria, tuberculosis, measles, polio, mumps, scarlet fever and whooping cough, all of which flourished in areas of poor sanitation. Those who lived in poverty, were ill-nourished or weak, succumbed quickly to these diseases. Overcrowded conditions in Underground stations and public shelters compounded the problem. Childhood epidemics were the chief cause of infant mortality and far surpassed the impact of bombing in terms of the number of fatalities. Diphtheria was by far the biggest killer in children under the age of 10, and although it was possible to immunise children against diphtheria, opposition from an anti-vaccination league and local authorities thwarted initial government attempts to eradicate the disease. There was also a 45 per cent rise in cases of non-pulmonary tuberculosis (brucellosis) in children caused by untreated milk. Children living in London were supplied by London dairies; Express Dairies and United Dairies supplied milk to other cities. These dairies provided good-quality pasteurised milk, whereas children living in rural areas were drinking untreated milk and suffered the consequences.[11]

Yet some sections of the population were benefitting from medical discoveries and treatments that had been made during the 1930s, and were being implemented on a wider scale during the war. Childhood diabetes was being treated with insulin injections for the first time, thanks to scientific discoveries made by Banting and Best. Wider medical screening for children identified health problems associated with venereal diseases before they were born. New treatments were introduced to combat pernicious and simple anaemia, and health education programmes were beginning to have an impact. Wartime rationing did not permit extravagant daily menus, but extra milk was made available for pregnant women. Moreover, Ministry of Health officials focussed considerable attention on improving care for babies and infants under 5, and survival rates for babies increased.[12]

Notes

1 'Danger in Safety', *Daily Mirror*, 5 October 1940, p. 2.

2 'Heroes of the Blitz', quoted in *British Journal of Nursing, New York Times*, November 1940, p. 196.

3 Walker, A., Oral history testimony, Imperial War Museum Sound Archives ref: 17977/2/1-2.

4 *British Journal of Nursing*, Disciplinary Cases, November 1940, p. 191. Please note that Aero factory refers to the Austin Aero factory based in Birmingham.

5 London Metropolitan Archives, Matrons' Report Book ref: H01/ RW/C/01/003, 1 October 1940.

6 *Ibid.*, Matron's Report Book, 29 October 1940.

7 *Ibid.*

8 Starns, P., *Nurses at War* (2000), p. 6.

9 *Ibid.*, p. 6–7.

10 Clark-Kennedy, A.E., *London Pride: The Story of a Voluntary Hospital* (1979), pp. 19–20.

11 For further information, please see Hansard House of Commons Parliamentary Debates, 5th Series, 30 June 1942, vol. 385, col. 137. The last case of brucellosis in Britain was diagnosed at the Bath and Wessex Orthopaedic Hospital in 1972. The 7-year-old boy had been drinking infected untreated milk on his parents' farm in Somerset; he made a successful recovery due to powerful antibiotic medication that was not available during the war.

12 Starns, P., *Blitz Families: The Children who were Left Behind* (2012), Chapter 5: Childhood Epidemics, pp. 61–73.

7

NURSING THE ENEMY

At 3 a.m. on 28 October 1940, the Italian Ambassador issued an ultimatum to General Metaxas, the Prime Minister of Greece. Mussolini requested permission to invade Greece unopposed or he would declare war on the Greek people. Metaxas replied, 'Then it is war.'[1] Greece was an important British ally and had allowed the Royal Navy access to ports in the Eastern Mediterranean. On 9 November, Churchill declared:

> there is one heroic country to whom our thoughts today go out in new sympathy and admiration. To the valiant Greek people and their armies, now defending their native soil from the latest Italian outrage – to them we send from the heart of old London our faithful promise that amid all our burdens and anxieties we will do our best to aid them in their struggle, and we will never cease to strike at the foul aggressor in ever increasing strength from this time forth until the crimes and treacheries which hang around the neck of Mussolini, and disgrace the Italian name have been brought to condign and exemplary justice.[2]

However, in addition to providing support for the Greeks, British forces were beginning a long struggle for control of North Africa and the Middle East.

Royal Air Force squadrons were doing their best to protect British cities and industrial areas, but shorter days and longer nights favoured incoming German bombers. Moreover, in London and the Home Counties nurses were given a new and most unpleasant challenge – that of nursing the enemy. German pilots shot down over the English Channel or London frequently sustained multiple fractures. Matrons and ward sisters stressed the universality of medicine and the need to view German patients as 'just another case'. This was easier said than done. Monica Dickens noted:

> Nurse Dawlish said in her slow, resentful voice, 'after all they did come here to drop bombs on us. I don't see how we are expected to forget that. I think it's an awful cheek to expect us to nurse them. I shall give my notice in tomorrow. I didn't come her to toady to the Nazis.'[3]

Ward sisters instructed nurses to keep German patients a secret from British patients, and to keep them permanently hidden behind two sets of screens. As Monica further recorded, this was an impossible task:

> It didn't make any difference. The men found out within a day. One of the up patients kept sneaking behind the screens to 'see what the bleeders looked like.' It was all rather embarrassing. The two Germans were quite pleasant, well-mannered boys, not too badly injured to be perfectly aware of the effect of their presence on fellow patients. Naturally they hated being here as much as we hated having them. They both had fractures and were difficult to move, and anything one had to do for them, like bathing them or making their bed, took a long time. I suppose if I had been a good nurse I should not have grudged this time, but I did. Whenever the men saw one going behind the screens, they would yell out: 'Cut his bleeding throat, Nurse;' and other suggestions. The night nurse said it was dreadful at night when

there was an air raid. The men had never taken much notice before except to curse sleepily, but now they would all wake up to hurl abuse over the screens, and the Germans would lie blushing and silent, contemplating the irony of having a bomb dropped on them by their own side.[4]

In some instances, German pilots were nursed in the same hospital wards as their victims. Occasionally, German patients were remarkably compliant. But there were others who deliberately urinated or defecated their beds, pulled out their wound drains and intravenous drips, and adopted a truculent manner towards those trying to care for them. National press reports highlighted these disturbing incidents, whilst the nursing profession was divided as to the best way to deal with them:

> The notes by Mr Beverley Nicholls, which are a popular feature of the *Sunday Chronicle*, reported recently that a nurse had been spat upon by a German prisoner, and did the right thing in walking away and ignoring the insult. From the correspondence to which this gross, but characteristic, conduct gave rise, his opinion was not unanimously approved. Mrs A. Townsend, of Bridlington, York, wrote: 'I should have slapped his face very good and hard.' That is the Yorkshire way, straight from the shoulder joint and make no mistake about it. We nurses, however, approve of our colleagues' dignified conduct, but the less we are called upon to associate with barbarians, the better.[5]

For the most part, nurses ignored insults from German patients, and there were even cases where nurses had reputedly fallen in love with the enemy. Those who fraternised with Germans, however, were instantly dismissed. Amongst those who lost their jobs and were brought before the courts were: Sister Margaret Mulvena, aged 37; Sister Winnie Cunnane, aged 31; and Nurse Ivy Nott, aged 21. Along with two probationer nurses, these women were accused of communicating with German prisoners of war and sending them gifts. All were found guilty and the registered nurses were fined. No action was taken against the two probationer nurses.

It was reported in the press that, with one exception, these women were Irish! Consequently the nursing press continued to highlight the difficulties of caring for the enemy and strongly cautioned nurses against fraternising with their German patients. Editorials in the *Journal of British Nursing* consistently reminded nurses of the nightly devastation wreaked on London and elsewhere as a result of enemy action:

> Fires once more raged in the city, after the indiscriminate showering of incendiary bombs by the barbarous enemy, which was the fiercest fire-raising attempt of the war, in which historic Guildhall and eight of Wren's churches were destroyed. We specially grieve the loss of lovely St Bride's, Fleet Street, with its slender spire, the journalists' own church. St Paul's Cathedral ringed by fires was in danger for some time. Bombs fell on and burnt through the lead roofing, but were extinguished before serious damage could be done. For miles away the Cathedral stood out clearly against a glowing sky.[6]

Righteous indignation.

The Rev. F. C. Baker the devoted Vicar of St Stephen's Coleman Street, expressed the feelings of all of us who have been privileged to serve the City of London, as nurses have done for centuries. In an address to St Margaret's Lothbury he said: 'The church is down but my blood is up. It is up with righteous indignation, and I hope I am none the less a Christian for it. As I stood on the ashes of St Stephen's Church this morning I thought of Christ's denunciation of Capernaum: Thou Capernaum, which art exalted to heaven shalt be thrust to hell. I feel sure that if Christ were standing in this City today that is what he would say about Germany. I have read much history in my time, but I know of no nation so depraved, so hellish and brutal as Germany has proved herself to be; for it is not Hitler alone, but the German nation which has endorsed his methods which must be held responsible when the day of reckoning comes.

He was amazed he said, that such persons as pacifists or conscientious objectors could be found in such days as these. There was nothing

Christ-like about their attitude. Christianity was not for milksops, but for men and women ready to restrain evil wherever it existed. Pacifist and conscientious objectors were assisting Hitler just in the way he wanted help by refusing to join battle against him.[7]

Yet as Rose confessed to her diary, conscientious objectors often played a significant part in the war effort, even though they refused to kill:

A dozen of us attended a tea dance yesterday in the town hall. We drank stewed tea served with thick bread covered in sloppy parsnip and beetroot jam. It was a foul, semi liquid liberally poured onto bread. Gladys says we will just have to get used to the taste, in other words – it was disgusting. The tea was not much better – so dark and thick you could almost stand your spoon up in it! Not that we needed a spoon because there was no sugar. I was just thinking that I ought to be polite and drink it anyway when I was rescued by a rather dashing young man called Harold who asked me to dance. He's serving with the R.A.M.C. [Royal Army Medical Corps] and positively hates the war. He told me he believes in saving lives not taking them, I think he's probably a conchie [conscientious objector] but still seems to want to do his bit. I told him he needs to be careful what he says. We've been bombed to smithereens and feelings are running high, folk round here give conchies a sound bashing. He says he'll be alright – after all he is in uniform, he's not a shirker conchie. While we were doing a slow dance he pulled me very close. I hoped he might say something romantic but he simply asked if the bakery on Barking Road was still open! Town hall care taker standing nearby overheard him – before I could open my mouth, he tapped him on the shoulder 'it's more open than usual mate – whole bloody shop front's been blown away!' This made him throw back his head with laughter. He's very handsome, tall and quite charming. His shiny black hair isn't all slicked back with grease like some, and he has twinkling brown eyes and a cheeky grin. He made me promise faithfully to write to him, and I will when I have time. Goodness only knows when I'll see him again. This wretched war is a darn nuisance. One things for sure, I won't tell anyone Harold's a conchie, not even Glad [Gladys Tyler].

Rose's friend Gladys was attempting to read Jane Austen's *Persuasion* in their shared bedroom. Slamming doors accompanied by noisy chatter as probationers changed shifts, congregated in corridors to catch up on gossip or made their way to washrooms interrupted her thoughts. It was useless to tell them to be quiet. They would speak in hushed tones for a few minutes and then forget, their voices rising gradually, interspersed with bouts of giggling or raucous laughter. Since they had spent their long working hours rigidly suppressed by hospital etiquette, they desperately needed to let their hair down. It was only when Gladys was reading that she found such noise a source of irritation. Often she found it comforting – a life-affirming cacophony of energy and youth. She felt certain that even in the austere-looking nurses' home there was more freedom than in Jane Austen's day. Gladys was quite convinced that all young women needed to be well educated. Devouring long-established novels and poems, like listening to classical music, was all part and parcel of Gladys' quest for sophistication. She had made herself a list of books, which included the complete works of Shakespeare, Jane Austen and Charles Dickens, and was determined to wade through them with tenacity. On completion of this daunting task she intended to read the works of ancient philosophers, although she had absolutely no idea what philosophy meant. In fact, her diary indicated that she was already beginning to tire of Jane Austen:

I find her language too flowery and she seems to take forever to get to the point. Yet I must read her books because parts are very witty and clever. I can learn so much from her and once I've worked through my list I will surely have an ability to hold forth on many subjects. Mother tells me I'm far too serious but how else am I to learn? I'm not entirely sure if I want to be a nurse. I have an inkling that after the war there will be more opportunities for us (women) to do all sorts of jobs. Nursing is fine for now but I'd like to travel and see a bit of the world. One of our patients is in the merchant navy and he's been everywhere. He loves his way of life and talks incessantly about exotic lands, beautiful sunsets, fascinating people and interesting food. Of course the blasted war has changed everything, but it won't last forever.

Gladys' wanderlust was also fuelled by letters she received from an old school friend named Ivy, who, upon joining the Queen Alexandra's Imperial Military Nursing Service, was travelling the world.

Dear Glad,

I planned to tell you all about our work and location, but all our letters are heavily censored so I cannot tell you everything. I can tell you that I am working with what the men call the vampire vans! These are small mobile refrigerated vans that take blood to all units. We take blood from troops and it is stored in some kind of centrifugal refrigerator. In some cases blood is separated into plasma and packed cells. This is quite new and means that it can be stored for longer. Some of our patients do not need volume you see, so packed cells gives them iron and such without putting too much fluid into their bodies. Plasma is glorious because it stays fresher for longer than whole blood. Advances in this field are extraordinary and transfusions save lives every single day. Sometimes we get a bit short of blood but not for long. The troops are very generous in donating blood. They never know when they might need some you see. I am not allowed to tell you where we are, only that it is scorching hot, and the place is covered in flies. We have abandoned the wearing of white caps and aprons because the washing water is brown. No matter how much soap is used all white clothes are tinged a dirty brown colour. Nights are extremely blustery and dust gets everywhere. Nobody wears stockings anymore. I cannot tell you much about our casualties, but a by-product of hoards [sic] of flies is that all wounds are infested with maggots. I know this must sound frightfully revolting but maggots eat decayed flesh and the wounds heal amazingly well. I am sorry I cannot tell you more, but be assured that I am happy, working hard and enjoying every minute of it. Our medical unit has travelled a great deal. I would not have missed this for the world.

Gladys had wanted to enlist, but chose to stay and help her mother care for her dying father. There were many times, however, when she wished that her circumstances were different. Now her mother needed help to raise her younger sisters, and she always felt a twinge of envy reading Ivy's letters.

Folding her letter in two, she placed it in her diary to act as a bookmark. Christmas was fast approaching and she had done little in the way of preparation for the festive season. A combination of rationing and paper shortages limited the type of presents she could provide. She was not a gifted needlewoman and had no real aptitude in the kitchen. At a loss over what she could give to her mother and sisters, she decided to make some home-made make-up from petroleum jelly and beetroot juice. This became a rather messy affair, with Gladys trying out multiple combinations of liquids in her attempt to produce little glass pots of home-made lipstick.

Across at St Thomas', Grace, whose mind was never far from food, was studying the dietary requirements of her patients:

Milk diet – includes toast, bread and butter and eggs in their lightest form, as well as milk puddings.

Fluid diet – includes meat extracts and broths as chicken and beef tea, egg flips and barley water, as well as milk.

Light diet – includes fish, tripe, sweetbreads, and eggs.

Ordinary diet – consists of any of the usual articles of food, and it should be remembered that tongue, boiled mutton, a grilled chop or fillet steak are fairly easily digestible. The diet may be ordered which excludes root vegetables and starchy foods, or which excludes or limits flesh foods, or it may permit of thickened fluids only, or cool drinks only, or any variation whatever. For assuaging thirst, water, soda,

Imperial drink, tea and coffee are refreshing. Imperial drink is made from one lemon, one tablespoon of sugar, one teaspoon of tartar and one pint of boiling water. Allow to cool before serving.[8]

Grace wrinkled her nose in disgust at the thought of serving tripe, and seriously doubted whether any patients were served with fillet steaks in these days of rationing. Medical journals were extolling the virtues of milk, nuts and lentils as an alternative protein source, even though some patients found the latter indigestible. Grace made copious notes about foodstuffs for gastric patients before switching her attention to a Christmas cake recipe. This was to be her main contribution to family festivities and a gift to her hard-working mother, who spent all of her free time with the Women's Institute. She had been saving up dried fruit for the purpose and was reasonably confident of getting eggs from the chickens which roamed in the back yard. She would make some marzipan from semolina, water, a little sugar and soya. There would only be a small gathering this year. Her four older brothers were away fighting and it was unlikely they would get leave for Christmas. Most people were in similar circumstances. Grace thought, wistfully, that it wasn't the rationing that made the prospect of Christmas seem grim, but the absence of so many loved ones.

Flo, meanwhile, was knitting frantically in her off-duty hours. A shortage of wool had thwarted her initial efforts to produce home-made Christmas gifts. However, she resolved the problem by unpicking and unravelling wool from two of her old blue cardigans. These she managed to transform into two respectable-looking waistcoats, one for her father and another for Archie. Throughout the previous months she had knitted a bright red hat and scarf for her mother, adorned with a white knitted daisy, and pretty socks for all of her sisters, three of whom were clerks in the Auxiliary Territorial Service (ATS), whilst her youngest sister was an ambulance driver. Her two brothers worked as ground crew in the RAF. Flo had decided to give them knitted vests.

Matron Hillyers was busy organising Christmas entertainment schedules and gifts for St Thomas' patients, along with traditional carol services. Christmas trees were installed in basement wards, whilst haphazard paper chains made from painted recycled newspapers were glued together with flour and water paste to adorn ceilings and corridors. Stoical Londoners carried festive decorations into Underground stations, along with Christmas trees and handmade stockings for children. The national press, meanwhile, appealed to women to appreciate their menfolk and emphasise their femininity. An article published on Christmas Eve, featuring a photograph of a glamorous young woman dressed in underwear, was entitled: 'I'm hanging up my Christmas stocking and this is what I'm putting in it for myself!' Contents of her stocking were revealed as follows:

A doll ... to remind myself that whatever we grown-ups lack, we must make this the finest Christmas ever for the kiddies.

A toy rifle ... to remind me to smile back at the kit loaded soldier who grins at me. Probably his Christmas will consist of standing in dark trains for hours. And if a smile can cheer him up he'll get it.

An orange ... to remind myself that it's thanks to the men on cargo ships that I can still revel in the colours and the sweetness of the things they bring me.

A pen ... to remind myself to keep in touch with my friends, and that they will need cheering up as much as I do sometimes.

A money box ... to remind myself to save all I can for victory.

A powder puff ... to remind myself that though there mayn't be as much powder as there used to be, Hitler's no excuse for a perpetually shiny nose.

A bright new sixpence ... to remind myself that there is a silver lining to everything, thanks to the boys in blue, khaki and sky blue.

A balloon ... to remind myself that hot air's dangerous, whether I talk it or listen to it.

A heart shaped locket ... for His photograph, to remind me that his heart belongs to me, and mine to him.

A toy dumb-bell ... to remind myself that a fit Briton is a victorious Briton.

A photograph of Mr Churchill … to remind myself to work to the best of my ability, and that as long as I do England will always be free.

A toy watch … to remind myself to be punctual at my work, as time is as vital to our war effort as manpower, guns and aeroplanes.

A toy pair of spectacles … to remind myself that it is dangerous to view things through rose tints.

A candle … to remind myself that one day the lights of Europe will be relit and the world happy and at peace again.[9]

Alongside morale-boosting articles, newspapers also published guidelines for food prices, as laid down by Lord Woolton, the Minister of Food:

Prices of Christmas Fare

Some goods are controlled. Be careful, don't pay more than the prices Lord Woolton has fixed.

Uncontrolled:

Fish (per lb) – fresh haddock 1s 6d to 1s 8d; cod 2s to 2s 6d; lemon sole (small) 2s; halibut 3s 6d; hake 2s 6d; turbot 2s 9d.

Poultry – chickens 2s 8d; ducks 2s to 2s 3d; geese 1s 9d.

Controlled:

Rabbits are controlled at 9d or 11d a lb, skinned and cleaned.

Pork – home killed leg 1s 6d lb; imported 1s 3d lb, home killed middle cut 1s 8d lb, imported 1s 6d lb, mutton (legs) 1s 6d lb to 1s 10d lb, imported, 1s to 1s 2d lb.

Nuts are scarce, but you may be able to get brazils and hazels. Her are fair prices for them: brazils 1s 3d lb; hazels 9d lb. If you can find any oranges remember that Lord Woolton has fixed the price at 5½d lb.[10]

Most people did the bulk of their shopping on Christmas Eve to ensure food purchases were fresh. Pork was the meat of choice for many families, because there was a shortage of turkeys. Ministry of food recipes were widely available in the press and broadcast on radio. People were urged not to write too many Christmas cards because of a paper shortage, and they were also urged not to travel.

Mr J.C. Moore-Brabazon, Minister of Transport, issued a Christmas message to the nation:

> I wish I could be Santa Claus this Christmas and produce out of the bag hundreds of extra trains, miles of additional track and thousands of extra railway workers, so that you could travel where and as you wish – and in comfort. Instead I have to curtail Christmas passenger trains and try to persuade you not to travel at all. You know this must be a stern Christmas-tide – one during which we must work for victory. The enemy won't wait while we take a Christmas holiday and therefore railways must continue to devote all their energies to vital war transport. No extra holidays for railway workers – for you no extra travelling facilities. Forgive no presents this year, but best wishes for Christmas and the New Year.[11]

On Christmas Eve, children across London, whether in shelters, Underground stations or hospitals, hung up their stockings as usual. Families, friends and neighbours huddled together to sing cheerful Christmas songs as the bombs rained down on the city. Adults prepared food and sweets for their families, and placed photographs of loved ones in prime position near lovingly decorated Christmas trees. Hospital routines were supplemented with religious services, poetry readings and amateur pantomimes. Nurses toured the basement wards by candlelight, singing carols to patients who were confined to their beds. Most were in good spirits despite their circumstances, as Rose wrote cheerfully in her diary:

> All patients joined in with the singing, humming along if they didn't know the words. Some put in requests for certain carols and we did our best to oblige. There were twenty of us singing and our tour of the wards took over three hours. My candle blew out on a few occasions – a draught of cold air persists in our corridors. Sister ended our tour on the men's ward by reading a poem by Patience Strong:

Let the Christmas spirit enter.
Hate not, judge not, nor condemn.
Open wide your heart's dark window.
To the star of Bethlehem.
Break the bread of joy and share it.
So that none shall go in need.
Pass along the word of blessing.
Praise the Christ in thought and deed.
Light the candles, hang the holly.
Let the kindly wish be penned.
Give the gift and speak the greeting.
To the stranger and the friend.

There was a most respectful silence for a brief moment, then one of the men called out 'Me Swanee rivers' (liver) giving me jip and the quack says I can't have any Christmas spirit.' Peals of laughter followed. Sister managed to keep a dignified silence and left the ward with her head held high.

I received a damp Christmas card and letter from Harold five days ago, but I've no idea where he is or when he will be home. Gladys has been reading a lot of nonsense as usual, and told me last night about ancient Christmas traditions. She says that kissing under the mistletoe came about because of some chap called Balder. It's all to do with legend. Balder was a son of Odin and Freya. Freya doted on her son and told all living things to protect him. But she didn't tell mistletoe about this, so a god called Loki killed Balder with mistletoe wood. Other gods restored Balder's life and mistletoe promised not to do any more harm. Mistletoe was placed in the keeping of Freya who was the Goddess of love, so now it is associated with kissing.

She started rattling on about myths surrounding holly bushes too, but by that time I was so sleepy I couldn't concentrate. I find Gladys strange sometimes, and she says she's never heard of Vivien Leigh. Fancy that! I swear the girl goes around in a dream world most of the time.

We did have a nice Christmas morning in the nurses' home though … homemade crackers, a few nuts and sweets. Gladys gave me a jar of odd smelling face cream, and I gave her a copy of *Bleak House* … for some reason she wants to read everything Dickens wrote. I told her, there's enough bleakness all around us these days, no need to read about it. We were both on an early shift and sang 'we wish you a merry Christmas' all the way to the dining room. Everyone determined to enjoy Christmas!

After work I walked home and spent Christmas night in our shelter. Mum says Dad has 'the Morrison crawl.' From what I can make out, Morrison's crawl is the name Dad's doctor has given to his lumbago. It seems to apply to anyone who has spent night after night crouched in a Morrison shelter. We took Christmas cake into shelter with us, and got through the night.

Matron Reynolds at The London and Matron Hillyers at St Thomas' had worked through Christmas without much respite. Both were focussing their attention on nursing issues, in particular on nursing shortages. Along with other matrons and senior nurses, they had been lobbying MPs for nursing advisors to be installed at the Ministry of Health. All agreed that drastic action was needed in order to avoid a complete collapse of civilian nursing services. As Christmas festivities subsided, they expressed their concerns yet again to the Ministry of Health. This time with some degree of success. Meetings were held between nurse leaders and politicians, with the latter reluctantly admitting that their overall concern had been for quantity of nurses, not quality. Belatedly, they asked for nursing advice and as the end of the year approached, senior nurses prepared to enter Whitehall.

Notes

1 General Metaxas is reputed to have also said '*Oxi*', the Greek word for 'no'. Greeks celebrate Oxi Day every year on 28 October, with military parades, parties and family reunions.

2   Churchill, W., speech delivered at the Mansion House, London, during Lord Mayor's luncheon on 9 November 1940.
3   Dickens, M., *One Pair of Feet* (1942), p. 163.
4   *Ibid.*, pp. 163–64.
5   *British Journal of Nursing*, November 1940, p. 185.
6   *British Journal of Nursing*, January 1941, p. 3.
7   *Ibid.*
8   Matheson, G.J., *Sick Nursing for Girl Guides* (1934), pp. 22–23.
9   *Daily Mirror*, 24 December 1940.
10 *Ibid.*
11 Moore-Brabazon, J.C., MC, MP. A Christmas message to the nation broadcast by BBC, 24 December 1940.

THE SECOND GREAT FIRE OF LONDON

As 1940 drew to a close, British and Commonwealth forces were still standing firm against the Axis powers. For some time, British troops had been playing a cat-and-mouse game with the Germans and Italians across the deserts of North Africa and the Middle East. However, in December, under the leadership of Sir Richard O'Connor, three Italian camps were demolished and over 40,000 prisoners captured. The Italians were also coming under siege in Greece, where they were meeting with unexpectedly high levels of resistance. On the beleaguered Home Front, the Blitz continued. Indeed, 29 December 1940 was one of the fiercest nights of aerial bombardment; an attack which set the whole of London ablaze. St Guy's Hospital was one of many buildings to suffer the tremendous wrath of the Luftwaffe.

The first high-explosive bomb blasted through a subway between two buildings, destroying the massage building. Within seconds, the hospital grounds were lit up by incendiaries and the nurses' home roof was ablaze. A large building known as Hunts House and Bright's House Annexe caught alight and threatened a whole series of other structures. Mr Walter Bentley, resident engineer and assistant clerk of the works, recounted the event:

An odd thing followed the first bomb as the switchboard main breakers were thrown in not out as you might expect. This put on all the lights. There was a frantic rush to the generating station. To have all lights on with the enemy overhead was clearly not desirable. Though the sky was lit up by incendiaries anyway. Very soon a high explosive fell on the hospital hitting one of the oldest buildings – Dorcas ward, part of original Guys building in 1725. Then Martha ward heaved up. All patients were in the basement and no-one was hurt. Further bomb blasts followed. Fires increased in intensity. Police requested evacuation of hospital but only two roads were open to ambulances and one might be closed by fire at any moment. Steps were taken at once to carry patients to a rest centre outside zone of fire. Students worked like galley slaves, wrapping up sick people and carrying them to ambulances which the police provided. Some nurses went with patients. Others remained behind. Casualties not coming in because approach to hospital too difficult. Then worst of troubles began. The wind changed and freshened as it did so. Before we knew what was happening, over the flaming area outside our walls the whole park and hospital were obliterated by a snow storm of fire sparks. I don't know how else to describe it. They were so thick and constant that any man who had gone out without his tin hat would have had his hair catch fire. Then a miracle happened! When things looked their worst, the wind veered round once more and it began to rain. All clear sounded. Then a new fire on roof of Hunts House and a hard fight to put it out. Everything finally settled by 3am on 30th December.[1]

Referred to by Londoners as the Second Great Fire of London, this horrific attack inflicted severe damage to the city's infrastructure. Yet, in the midst of swirling palls of smoke and gigantic walls of flames, St Paul's Cathedral miraculously dominated the landscape, saved from destruction by specialist teams of firefighters. Furthermore, iconic photographs of Wren's historic cathedral, standing majestically above the devastating scenes of carnage, uplifted the nation and became symbolic of Britain's fight against evil.

As London hospitals attempted to clear debris-strewn pathways and grounds, salvaging furniture and equipment, matrons efficiently conducted their usual rounds. Offering calm reassurance to both patients and staff, they carried on with their duties, seemingly unperturbed by recent events. New Year's Eve was a subdued affair, with small beers for male patients and minute tots of sherry for female patients. For off-duty nurses, toasting time was enjoyed with cocoa as normal, but with an extra ration of jam. Grace recorded in her diary:

It doesn't feel much like New Year but it certainly feels like January. This morning there was a bitterly cold East wind and a slight sprinkling of snow on pavements below. A frosting of thick ice covers the inside of our windows, which Flo cheerfully dismisses as 'Jack Frost being about.' She doesn't seem to feel the cold as others do, but takes great pleasure in knitting woolly garments to keep her friends warm. I am grateful every night, as my feet are warmed by woolly socks she knitted me for Christmas. Gifts were sparse this year and mother spent Christmas day close to tears because none of her boys were home. I was relieved to get back to work. I've just moved to women's medical and I'd forgotten how much women natter, about all manner of things. Mrs Phillips in bed 3 says she's a martyr to her stomach, but she puts away all the food we give her without a hint of discomfort. Mrs Hodges in bed 14 is quite glamorous and was absolutely shocked to pieces to discover that I don't possess a lipstick. She gave me the most sympathetic look. Mrs Rogers in bed twenty is an entertaining sort. The other day she said to me, 'Nurse, I went to me quack because me usband keeps talkin in is sleep. Quack says lots of men are talking in their sleep on account of the blitz straining their nerves. Told me that if me usband goes to see im e can give im pills to quieten im down a bit. I says, I don't wan im to go quiet, I want pills to make him talk louder so's I can ere what he's saying!' With her story complete, patients in nearby beds laughed so loudly I had to scold her. But I have to confess I do have a soft spot for her. To be able to make people laugh in these grim times is something of a Godsend.

I was hoping we might see a better variety of food this year, but it seems we are to be stuck with the same old things. Lord Woolton says that potatoes, fresh vegetables, dried eggs and cheese should be regarded as staple foods for the time being. He also wants everyone to eat an extra cabbage during next month as there is an abundance of green vegetables this season. Mrs Rogers says, if we're not careful we're all going to look like cabbages!

Grace's friend Flo, meanwhile, remained on a male surgical ward, and could be found in off-duty hours, spread across her bed, reading a prize-winning paper on the recognition and treatment of surgical shock:

'Surgical' shock implies some traumatic element in its production, including that by operative surgery. It may be defined as a condition of dangerously low vitality, consequent upon some catastrophe, and its effect upon the nervous system, characterised by low blood pressure, subnormal temperature and shallow respirations, and accompanied by the typical picture of pallor, cold clammy skin, sunken eyes, feeble pulse, and general decrease in muscle tone. The mental accompaniment is usually one of apathy, unless the shock be due to haemorrhage, when restlessness and air hunger with great thirst will be present. Vomiting and rigor may occur – consciousness is not usually lost. Metabolic activity is low and various vascular phenomena have been demonstrated in recent findings.

Slight shock usually responds to rest in the recumbent position. Warmth and quiet, and warm fluid given by mouth if possible – if not, by rectum. Warm, sweet tea is considered safe in most cases – (alcohol is contraindicated where there is likelihood of bleeding) – and reassurance aimed at. The raising of the lower part of the body by blocks under the foot of the bed may help. Where hot water bottles have been inserted these must be carefully examined for soundness – correctly stoppered and covered, and anchored – particularly where the bed is on the slant. Medical assistance will be required. Severe shock will necessitate sterner measures. Blood transfusion or plasma transfusion, relief of pain by sedatives, saline infusions – the constant attendance of the nurse, and the most careful carrying out of all doctor's instructions – the oxygen tent or administration of warmed moistened oxygen by intranasal methods and of saline if given intravenously, the introduction of gum acacia or other colloid substance, to prevent osmosis into the tissues too rapidly.[2]

Flo concentrated hard as she tried to commit the article, eloquently written by Maggie Neal, to memory. Like all other probationers, Flo was forced to study in her off-duty hours, and attend nurses' lectures. This educational practice, along with poor pay, and petty restrictions, which governed a nurse's private and working life, were major obstacles to nurse recruitment. Furthermore, although ministers at Whitehall had belatedly asked senior nurses for advice, civilian nursing services were already on the brink of collapse. Civilian health was suffering as a result of nursing shortages, prompting hospitals in some areas to close their doors. In a desperate attempt to resolve the problem, three Chief Nursing Officer posts were created at Whitehall: the first at the Ministry of Health, the second at the War Office and the third at the Colonial Office. These newly appointed nursing officers persuaded the government to adopt a three-pronged approach to the problem. As a result, the role of the Civil Nursing Reserve (CNR) was no longer restricted to the emergency services, but extended to include all areas of nursing. The War Office took steps to return senior nurses to their respective hospitals on request, if these institutions were experiencing difficulties in filling senior positions, and the Ministry of Health insisted that all hospitals paid their own nurses at the same rate as nurses working for the CNR.

These measures narrowly succeeded in averting a total collapse of the nursing services, but had a limited effect. The extension of the CNR role improved staffing levels in most general hospitals, but the sanatoriums and mental institutions remained understaffed. Most CNR nurses did not want to nurse in the sanatoriums in case they actually caught tuberculosis, whereas mental nursing was considered to be more of a man's job, since, before the widespread use of tranquilisers, psychiatric patients frequently needed to be physically restrained. Steps taken by the War Office to return senior nurses to their civilian hospitals were largely ineffective. The time lapse between making a request to the War Office and receiving the released nurse tended to be a period of at least six months, because senior nurses who had joined the armed forces were often overseas. It was, therefore, virtually impossible to locate and return these nurses. Government intervention in the CNR salary issue, however, did have the desired effect, namely that of keeping regular hospital nurses in their positions. Nevertheless, hospitals were not going to pay their nurses at the same rate as those employed by the government's CNR without some form of compensation. Thus, the Ministry of Health had little option but to fund part of the salaries of all hospital nurses. By doing so, it became the largest employer of nurses, and henceforth had a vested interest in nursing issues.[3]

Matron Mabel Reynolds and Matron Gladys Hillyers were considered to be amongst the more enlightened, progressive matrons. Both expressed a keen interest in the welfare of their probationers and recognised the need for changes in nurse education. But there were others who steadfastly clung to old, outmoded traditions, and exerted intolerable levels of discipline on young probationers. Therefore, improvements in nurse salaries did very little to improve recruitment. A shortage of nurses also prompted newspapers to publish information instructing the general public on how they could care for people at home. An advisory 'Sister Clare' attempted to encourage young women to join the nursing profession, whilst simultaneously writing reams of useful practical tips for women looking after invalids:

You are needed as a nurse

A good nurse has a hundred and one devices and dodges up her sleeve, and she fishes them down as often as they're needed to add to her patient's comfort, or hasten his recovery. To slip a fresh pillow under his head instead of merely turning over his own is one, so always keep a pillow by the bedside for the purpose, and change the covers as often as you can.

An ordinary sheet folded lengthways and placed across the bed over the bottom sheet will ensure that he has a cool spot to lie on as often as you care to draw a little of the sheet through, first one way then the other, tucking the long ends neatly under the mattress.

Most people find it impossible to drink lying down, and there's not always a feeding cup available to make this easier. Three inches of rubber tubing on the end of a teapot spout solves that difficulty though.

Where there's been any injury to the mouth or lips, offer all fluid food in a tumbler and let your patient drink through a straw. He won't forget you for this little dodge.

A four hourly rub with methylated spirits or cheap eau de cologne and then a dusting of powder, will keep that little bone at the bottom of the spine from feeling numb and sore while lying or sitting in bed. Do it also to elbows and heels.

A dab of weak peroxide of hydrogen is the best thing in the world to unstick a dressing.

A bolster rolled in a sheet and placed under the knees (professionally known as a 'donkey') is a blessing when your patient begins to sit up.

A square hat box minus its lid one side will keep the pressure of the bed clothes off his feet, if you place it over them, on top of the top sheet and under the blankets.

Buy, hire or beg, an 'air ring' if you've not got one in the house. Blow it up half way, slip into a pillow case and let your patient lies on this if he is very bad, or likely to be in bed for more than a day or two.[4]

Weekly advice from 'Sister Clare' became required reading for home carers. Moreover, at a time when women were leaving traditional jobs to work as mechanics, tractor and ambulance drivers, farm hands and anti-aircraft gunners, newspapers became adept at reminding women that their first duty was still to the home and hearth. The perceived wisdom from a columnist named Dorothy Dix, for instance, reminded women:

It is just as much a woman's duty to make a comfortable home for a family as it is the man's job to provide the raw materials out of which the home is made. If every young man would find out before he gets married whether the girl whom he was about to entrust his stomach and his future comfort and happiness was a good cook and an expert with a broom, about half of the domestic misery in the world would be prevented, and more homes kept intact.[5]

According to the wisdom of Dorothy Dix if mothers comforted their children when they were ill or injured they were in danger of raising weaklings. One of her follow-up articles was entitled: 'Pity isn't good for you'. But Dorothy and those of her ilk were increasingly out of step with the lives of ordinary wartime women. Like the old-fashioned matrons who still ruled probationers with a rod of iron, Dorothy was desperately trying to impose traditional women's roles on a rapidly changing society. Labour shortages prompted the lifting of the marriage bar, so that women who had previously been required to resign on marriage were allowed to continue in employment. Retired teachers and nurses were coaxed out of retirement to supplement the workforce, and a plethora of nurseries enabled mothers with young children to work in munitions and other war-related work.

However, it was arguably nurses who were at the forefront of the Blitz in terms of dealing with injuries and fatalities. Bombing raids were intensifying, and on 11 January 1941, Bank Underground station received a direct hit, killing 111 people outright. Injuries were horrific. Sister Kathleen Raven was working at St Bartholomew's Hospital that night:

I think one of the worst nights for us, as regards pain, sorrow and death, was when bombs blasted through the Bank underground station, carrying the flaming debris right down to the platforms and burying the people taking refuge there, and burning them so as to be unrecognisable. Many many casualties were brought to us that night and I have never seen such burns in my life – black charred bodies, still alive. We had to do our best.[6]

Amidst a torrent of incendiaries and high-explosive bombs, rescue workers frantically tried to extricate victims:

There were terrible scenes when a high explosive bomb fell on a London subway, plunging through the surface and bringing the ruins crashing down on people who had taken refuge there. Many were killed. It was impossible yesterday to estimate the number of people who might still be trapped, but the bodies of a woman and two men were recovered. Rescue workers continued their search. The bomb dropped in the centre of a roadway which collapsed, and concrete slabs, a tarmac road surface and iron standards trapped those beneath. Men women and children staggered through the debris and were dragged out of the crater by helpers. One child who had lost her mother was crying and repeatedly asking for mummy. A small fire which broke out just underneath the surface was quickly put out but high explosives and incendiaries were still falling as the rescuers hacked their way through, by the light of torches to get out the wounded. The caretaker of a building opposite said 'girl ambulance drivers sat in their driving seats waiting to take the wounded to hospital. They had no protection from bombs or shrapnel.'[7]

The dead and wounded were taken to major London hospitals. Thirty were taken to The London, where Rose was on duty. She later described the scene in a letter to her aunt:

It was a desperate night, a scene from hell. I have never before seen such awful injuries, they were the stuff of nightmares. Stunned ambulance drivers constantly ferrying victims to and fro. People screaming, searching for loved ones, most of the injured could not be recognised. Many victims suffering from severe shock needed saline transfusions. Those who died on the way to hospital were stacked up in the grounds, there was no room in the mortuary to take all the bodies. The sight of men, women and children burnt black as coal will haunt me forever, so much wailing and distress. Lots of incendiaries dropped on the hospital roof, but our fire fighters dealt with them. We were so busy trying to treat the injured we took little notice when the hospital shuddered, and there was no time at all to comfort the dying. I am sorry to have to write to you of all this, and I know other cities are being bombed too, but it feels as though London has had more than its fair share. Two of our nurses have been taken ill in recent days with what the doctor calls siren strain, the rest of us are bearing up.

Rose's roommate Gladys also wrote of this disastrous night in her diary:

We've had a weekend of incendiaries and high explosives, some of the fire fighters say we've had oil bombs too, but I'm not sure what they are. I have seen so many dead people in recent months, it has made me thankful my father died of natural causes. I stupidly thought I'd become used to seeing the worst of the raids, but the carnage at Bank underground has shocked and disturbed me far more than I thought possible. I'm not at all sure I'm cut out to be a nurse. I despair of my constitution. Sister says I'm no earthly good to anyone if I can't control my emotions.

Over at St Thomas', Flo and Grace were also struggling with the nature of their workload. In the aftermath of the Bank disaster, Flo was struggling to sleep. Grace, who always took a matter-of-fact approach to life, was outwardly calm and self-controlled, but confided to her diary: 'When I think of those dreadfully scorched poor souls I feel quite wobbly and I've not been able to eat a morsel for three days.'

Nurses, trained and untrained, dealt with their emotions as best they could. Most successfully suppressed their feelings in an attempt to instil courage in their patients. However, cadet nurses who joined the profession straight from school were extremely daunted when faced with a vast array of appalling injuries on a daily basis. These girls were only 15 years of age, yet they were expected to adapt to a furious pace of work and help with the treatment of casualties. Not surprisingly, the fall-out rate was high amongst this age group. However, by the end of January the Ministry of Health had managed to persuade 300 nurses to come out of retirement to work as nurses in Underground shelters. They received an inclusive salary of 3 guineas a week and they were required to work ninety-six hours a fortnight, involving alternate nights on duty whilst the hours of blackout were at their longest. Four part-time matrons were also appointed to visit and supervise nursing personnel in the shelters in consultation with medical officers.[8]

Members of the nursing profession broadly welcomed the policy of bringing state-registered nurses out of retirement, viewing this move as infinitely preferable to the introduction of second-grade enrolled nurses. The nursing press, meanwhile, as an antidote to the wisdom and dictates of Dorothy Dix, embarked on a crusade to highlight the historical significance of medical women:

In the seventeenth century, several titled ladies who had studied abroad, became well known, and a Hannah Woolley, of London, actually published a rather popular book on medicine. Whether remedies such as being 'laid in horse dung' for eighteen days were widely used cannot be said. In Scotland a Lady Anne Halkett acted as surgeon to the Royal Army, gaining the gratitude of James II for her services. The fact that few of the women mentioned above had university degrees does not detract from their skill as official and compulsory standards had never been established. Dorothea Christine Erxleben, however, received a medical degree from the university of Halle in 1741 and practised medicine for several years. Laura Bassi, lectured in anatomy at Bologna in the eighteenth century, while, in 1729, Antonia Elizabeth Von Held, although unqualified, proclaimed herself a specialist in the treatment of syphilis. Dr Charlotte Von Siebild, the daughter of a well-known midwife, obtained a degree in Gottingen and was known in England. One of the most interesting and striking discoveries in therapeutics was the introduction of digitalis by Withering. He described the subject of digitalis treatment fully, but the credit must be given to a medical woman of the eighteenth century, Mrs Hutton. Although she was unqualified she practised medicine and treated many well-known patients suffering from dropsy and heart disease.[9]

In an effort to aid recruitment, the Ministry of Health used historical stories of nurses' heroism to appeal to young girls. Propaganda constantly stressed Florence Nightingale's exploits in the Crimea and her pioneering work in establishing the first nursing schools at Netley and St Thomas'. The remarkable heroism of Edith Cavell, who trained at The London, and was shot during the First World War for helping soldiers to escape from the Germans, also featured prominently within the pages of nursing journals. But nursing could not compete with other occupations which offered more money for fewer hours. Ministry of Labour officials encouraged the national press to berate young women, who had opted for safety in the countryside, into action:

Security can be nothing much better than a prison. Thousands of protected young women are living in quiet country houses knitting. They would like to do something, but have no idea how to begin. The Services would fling them into rough conditions and they could not face that. Nursing would mean long hours on their feet and that would be difficult too. These secure young women are going to be bewildered and afraid and less safe than they have ever been in their whole lives in any worthwhile kind of future. They are going to feel the sting of competition and the whip of criticism, and listen to the easy, confident voices of young women who have lived on the edge of life since their school days and who take risks as they take bus rides. We have got to learn and to teach our youth, that security is not a set, traditional thing, something that can be given or taken away; that security is not 'everything the same' or a hundred per cent protection from every economic and emotional wind that blows. True security … the only kind that matters … is the ability to accept changes with self-confidence, to make the best of life and circumstance as it is.[10]

As press articles rallied to assist nurse recruitment, existing probationers struggled to combine work and study. Rose, Gladys, Flo and Grace had managed against the odds of punishing duty rotas to become firm friends, each one coping with extreme tiredness and stress. Grace had succumbed to buying Sanatogen nerve tonic, which promised to help the body retain phosphorous and improve nerve nourishment by 63 per cent. Gladys had turned to Ovaltine, to wipe away any signs of siren strain. Flo had opted to take Yeastvite, which she believed would give her extra energy; whilst Rose had rejected all types of tonic and pills, treating herself instead to a bar of Palmolive soap. All four were planning to get together for a special evening in March, to celebrate Rose's birthday. They had written formal requests for off duty to their ward and home sisters. None could be sure of getting the time off, but they lived in hope. In the meantime, they continued with their increasingly strenuous workloads and spent as much free time as possible studying for examinations.

Notes
1 Curnock, G.C., *Hospitals Under Fire* (1941), pp. 78–82.
2 Neale, M., 'What is surgical shock?', *British Journal of Nursing*, January 1941.
3 Starns, P., *Nurses at War* (2000), p. 28.
4 'You are needed as a nurse', *Daily Mirror*, 22 January 1941.
5 'Wisdom of Dorothy Dix', *Daily Mirror*, 12 March 1941.
6 Memoirs of Dame Kathleen Raven in Royal College of Nursing, *History of Nursing Journal*, vol. 3, no. 3 (1990), pp. 44–45.
7 *Daily Mirror*, 13 January 1941.
8 *British Journal of Nursing*, January 1941, p. 7.
9 *British Journal of Nursing*, February 1941, p. 34.
10 *Daily Mirror*, 12 March 1941.

9

PROLONGED AIR RAIDS

A bitter winter was followed by a crisp, frosty spring, and there was little respite for the Allies as Germany mounted a counteroffensive in North Africa. However, in the United States, President Roosevelt signed a Lend Lease Bill, which at least offered financial support for Britain's war effort. On the Home Front, improvements in radar systems resulted in better defences, but prolonged air raids took their toll on hospitals and their staff. In early March, The London was bombed for five hours, hospital lifts failed and bombs wiped out Bishopsgate telephone exchange. Consequently hospitals were unable to communicate with rescue workers, ambulance drivers, staff in the neighbouring area and patients' relatives. Ambulance drivers in particular experienced difficulties in ferrying patients to hospitals, although, surprisingly, neighbours took a keen interest in the arrival of ambulances at private homes during the Blitz, despite the risks of injury. A 20-year-old female ambulance driver noted when communications were restored:

> Our first call gave us a patient we didn't expect, a woman who was going to have a baby. Frightened by the bombing, she had to be taken to hospital at once. I have never seen anything like the scene

in the street. In spite of the bombs, women were standing at every door, asking each other what it was all about, why had the ambulance come? Who was going to be taken off? And so on. They followed the stretcher bearers into the house and were most anxious to help in moving our patient.

During the earlier weeks of the blitz we learned to be very grateful for our first aid training. We are not called on so often now to help in that way. There are more first aid workers, and in any case the most important thing is to get the victim quickly to a hospital. You don't want to keep people hanging about when there are bombs falling. We cover people up, see that they are comfortably fixed in the ambulance and take the smoothest road to the nearest hospital. That takes some finding on a black night, with the way possibly blocked by a fallen house or a new made crater.[1]

Facing a barrage of bombs, burst water mains, flaming gas and falling buildings, rescue parties using crowbars, shovels and often their bare hands also bore the brunt of the Blitz. Mr Weekes, who was a builders' labourer, and Mr Wilkins, a former carpenter, recounted:

There were steel shelters blown in and brick from the party wall all over the place. Tons and tons on the floor above. Ceiling gone in some places and many supports ready to give way. First thing we saw was a boy trapped by his toes under a pillar. His father was frantic because he couldn't shift it. The boy was a kid of twelve, and kept saying 'my leg hurts, my leg hurts.' Seeing it couldn't be done any other way, one of us said to the kid, 'You've got to do this on your own sonny. It may hurt but pull all you can.' So the kid gives just one 'Oh!' and out comes his foot. He had a bad crushed foot so we put him on a stretcher and took him to the pavement outside the post office.[2]

Moments later, another bomb fell directly outside a post office where the young lad had been taken for first aid. He was killed instantly, along with two Australians and a driver named Mr Bushel. The latter man was the driver of a second rescue party to appear on the scene, he was due to get married in a few days.

Mr Wilkins described another gruesome call-out to a public shelter:

There was a pillar interfering with the work. I went to get to puncheons (timber support). As I went I saw an overcoat and picked it up, thinking there might be someone under it. That was the first dead man I ever saw. Another thing I saw when I went up for the bases was a woman lying on the pavvy at the end of Brownlow street, just in front of the post office, with nothing on, and as black as a Newgates' knocker.[3]

One of the victims rescued by Wilkins and Weekes was a cold storage trundler named Frederick Grant. He had spent the day with his two adult sons, before taking refuge when an air raid siren sounded at 8 p.m. He spoke of his dramatic rescue whilst in hospital:

George my youngest, he's twenty five, was asleep in the corner, and that was the only place where it was really safe, as it turned out. Frederick Grant junior, he's twenty six and a trundler like myself – he was nearer me but not alongside. Must have been early in the morning when I woke up with the sounds of a bomb in my head. Junior went on sleeping. What happened to George I don't know. He got out. I was just wondering when we should get our lot, when it came. Being wide awake I saw the side of the wall going out and coming in again, and the steel columns bending, just like it might in a nightmare. I rolled over, and buried my head in my arms; the light went and I could feel the ceiling coming down, or perhaps it was mostly bricks from the wall. Anyway, there I was, with what on top of me I can't say, seeing that I was pinned down and choking with dust. When that was all over I couldn't get up to see what had happened to the boys. As I lay I heard two more bombs come down. I tried to call for help but couldn't do more than groan. So the next I recollect is that water is coming in through the ceiling and there's a smell of smoke. Now I know there is fire and water, so I begin to feel pretty certain I shall never get out alive because it's a plain case of being burned or drowned before they can get me. I can feel the water flooding the floor, and I try hard to get myself up a bit, all the time hoping it won't drown Fred. After a time I'm thankful to hear voices. Two men with a lantern got through but couldn't get me out. I was now able to lift up my head and could see Fred, who was lying there with his legs caught too, saying nothing, and looking like he's an awful mess because he's bleeding from his head. I remember thinking, perhaps if he isn't drowned the water might stop that a bit. There was some talk. A doctor got near enough to give me and Fred morphine. He said he thought they could get us out alright, but they wanted some tackle. I think I must have got sleepy after that because I can't remember how time went. I saw them lifting some big stuff off my boy, and by the time they had the piping, which was the steel columns off me it was 7am or later in the morning. As the bomb fell when it was dark, I suppose I was under the influence of Hitler, you might say, for about three hours. Now the doctor says I have nerves, but I think I'll still be able to do a bit of trundling, if that will help the war along.[4]

Frederick Senior and his eldest son were rushed to Great Ormond Street Hospital for emergency treatment, before being transferred to a sector hospital. By this stage, all major London hospitals had increased their quota of emergency beds, and during heavy raids they opened up more resuscitation rooms. Matrons were still run ragged trying to keep tabs on both London and sector hospitals, whilst nurses were now accustomed to having their duty rotas changed without warning. Medical staff previously injured in the autumn bombings were beginning to drift back to their hospitals, and those doctors who were in training, such as Dr Arthur Walker at St Thomas', were able to resume their studies. However, whilst medical education was evolving and improving, nurse education left a lot to be desired. Nurses in training were taught basic practical skills, but little theoretical knowledge. At The London, Lisbeth Hochsinger (Hockey), the alien ex-medical student, had been unable to resist the temptation to conduct nursing research on her patients, and had subsequently incurred the wrath of ward sisters on several occasions. Despite her lowly probationer nurse status, Hockey insisted on keeping meticulous notes on the treatment of bed sores during her various ward assignments. Different sisters used different methods, both to prevent bed sores from occurring and to treat existing sores. From egg white and oxygen to iodine and creams, there was no rhyme or reason to these treatments. Hockey was merely trying to establish the most successful methods. Her colleagues were at times amused by her efforts, and other times bewildered as to why she was bothering. Sisters dismissed her research, curtly reminding her that she was no longer a medical student, and pointing out that their personal nursing methods were the result of years of experience. Hockey, whose character was not restrained by English reserve, forcefully argued that she was unimpressed by nurses' lectures because they simply contained snippets of extremely diluted medicine. Within the confines of the nurses' home, it was not long before Hockey and her latest 'tango' with the nursing sisters became the subject of some renown.

Rose, meanwhile, who was primarily interested in nurse education in terms of passing exams, had completed her examination revision and was surveying herself in the mirror. A cursory look at her appearance confirmed the fact that she was looking less and less like Vivien Leigh as the weeks passed. Part of the problem, she decided, was her hair. She'd persuaded Gladys to trim it with some blunt-ended nursing scissors, but for some reason her curls were no longer behaving as they once did. She was approaching her 21st birthday, and convinced that she would end up an old maid, solemnly informed Gladys that she would be forever on the shelf because she hadn't heard from Harold in over a month. Rose was also suffering from cinema withdrawal symptoms. She had hoped to catch a showing of *The Philadelphia Story* starring Katherine Hepburn and Cary Grant. People were queuing round the block to see it at The Empire in Leicester Square. Cinema and theatre managers were extraordinarily good to nurses, and often sent complimentary tickets to the home sister for distribution to those who were off-duty. Rose was usually amongst the first to grab these tickets, but in recent weeks her duty rota had included lots of split shifts. With her usual route to escapism blocked, Rose began to lose some of her vibrancy. However, Gladys, Flo and Grace were secretly organising a special evening for her birthday – a meal at a West End restaurant, complete with a dance floor and jazz band. They enlisted the help of Rose's mother, who casually informed her daughter that family, friends and the whole neighbourhood would be coming to the family home for a 'knees up' on her birthday. Rose was not impressed by this idea of a 'knees up', confiding to her diary: 'I had in mind something altogether more glamorous for my coming of age celebration. I understand there is a war on, everyone keeps harping on about it, but Hitler should not be allowed to get in the way of people's birthdays.'

In their shared room, Gladys bore the brunt of Rose's disappointment, and was tempted to let the cat out of the bag on more than one occasion. However, Gladys was never one to break a confidence:

> We have arranged a delightful birthday surprise for Rose – in truth we all need a cheerful night out after tiresome months of night raids. I'm dog tired and have given up reading for the present. I simply cannot concentrate these days. We've all been doing domestic work in addition to our nursing jobs … it's just too much. Probationers are leaving in droves and there has been many a time when I have considered joining them.

Over at St Thomas', Florence and Grace were also excitedly looking forward to Rose's 21st birthday. In preparation, Florence began reworking her well-worn pale pink frock by adding bits of ancient Nottingham lace, procured from her grandmother's precious tablecloth. She had even bought a packet of 'Hiltone' blonde dye to brighten up her existing flaxen hair. Grace temporarily abandoned her Ministry of Food cookbooks in favour of curling her hair and rummaging around in her mother's dressing table for lipstick remnants. Members of her Girl Guide unit had presented her with a pile of frocks, all available on loan for an evening. Sifting through the colours and fabrics, Grace eventually chose an emerald green gown which suited her figure and complemented her eyes.

On the morning of 8 March, Rose awoke to Gladys bouncing on her bed like an excited puppy dog, and singing 'She's got the key of the door, never been 21 before!' Coaxing her friend to smile, Gladys presented her with a small pile of gifts: a dainty new powder compact from Florence, a bright Max Factor red lipstick from Grace and new metal curling clips from Gladys. All obtained with help of a spiv named Norman Atkins. As Rose unwrapped the small parcels, the prospect of a family knees up seemed less disagreeable. At least she had the day off and she could relish being the centre of attention. Once washed and dressed, however, Gladys sprang the surprise, explaining to Rose that her birthday plans were not going to be exactly as she had anticipated. There would be a family gathering in the afternoon, complete with birthday cake and home-made bunting, but in the evening she would need to put on her 'glad rags'. Rose squealed with glee and frantically searched the wardrobe for something suitable to wear, until Gladys knowingly informed her that an evening gown would be waiting for her at home.

At seven o'clock the friends met by Waterloo Bridge, and made their way to the West End in a rather undignified manner on the back of a horse-drawn cart. Grace's father was supposed to have driven them to their destination in a friend's jalopy, but a burst tyre had forced them to seek alternative transport – a neighbour's rag and bone cart. Nothing could dispel the sheer joy and excitement, however, of four young nurses dressed in all their finery, eager to dance the night away. Upon their arrival at the restaurant, they were greeted by the head waiter and shown to their table on a balcony. It was like entering a different world. Blackout curtains were concealed by plush, deep red velvet drapes, glistening chandeliers hung majestically from the ceiling, and a five-piece band played lively music from a raised platform near a smooth polished dance floor. Tables were covered in fine white linen tablecloths and the food was served from silver platters onto beautiful bone china. Men were formally attired in black dinner jackets and ties, whilst women were elegantly clothed in beautiful dresses adorned with sparkling jewellery. Temporarily cocooned from the outside world, they slowly consumed their food, engaged in light-hearted conversation, and twirled around the dance floor. Energetic, joyful tunes filled the air, along with peals of laughter, the rustling of stiff petticoats under sumptuous ball gowns, and the chinking of glasses. Rose, completely absorbed in her glamorous surroundings, was dressed in a long bright red gown, made from her grandmother's satin cotton wedding dress. Dyed and embellished with gold coloured beads, one of her mother's friends at the munitions factory had deftly interwoven small clusters of gold thread flowers around the neckline and waist.

Florence, in her pale pink lace-adorned dress, looking like a china doll, sat opposite Rose. Grace, in her emerald green, sat on her left, and Gladys, who had chosen to wear a simple frock of cornflower blue with cinnamon tulle, sat on her right. All were feeling young and carefree for the first time in months. Several gentlemen had asked them to dance, they had flirted, smiled and encouraged their attentions. War seemed a lifetime away – and then it returned, suddenly, dramatically, without warning. The packed dance floor received a direct hit – blood spilled over the dancers like a red flood. Scenes of carnage, choking dust, falling debris, screams and wails, smashed chandeliers, splintered glass blasted in all directions. Dazed, horrified, but unscathed, Rose and her friends moved swiftly about the restaurant giving comfort to the injured, pouring neat alcohol onto their wounds, and covering the dead with blood-splattered tablecloths. They tore strips from their petticoats to make bandages for the wounded, and tried to protect them as debris cascaded down. Five young women who been sitting near to the dance floor were killed outright. Twenty couples, gaily dancing only moments before the bomb descended, also lost their lives. Rescue workers were soon on the scene, and by the light of incendiaries worked desperately to save the injured. Rose, Gladys, Florence and Grace were amongst the last people to leave the wreckage, along with a Canadian nursing sister. Reports in the press praised the work of off-duty nurses:

A Canadian nursing sister was one of the heroines in a London restaurant which was bombed in Saturday night's raid. She worked in the bombed building among the dead and dying for more than an hour. She was Miss Helen Stevens of Dunnville, Ontario, who is now a nursing sister in No.1 Canadian General Hospital England. Canadians on weekend leave, British officers and men, and Londoners were dining in the restaurant when it was hit by a high explosive bomb. Miss Stevens went to the restaurant with a party of Canadians, including nursing sister Thelma Stewart of Toronto, her close friend, and Lieutenant Jack Clunie and Lieutenant Jack Wright, both of Sarnia, Ontario. When the bomb fell, Miss Stewart and Lieutenant Wright were dancing. Miss Stevens and Lieutenant Clunie, disliking the tune which was being played, went to their table in the balcony. Then the crash came. Wright, who was among the killed shielded Miss Stewart. 'This Canadian officer died protecting a Canadian nurse' said Miss Stevens. Clunie suffered minor wounds but has recovered. As the wounded called for help Miss Stevens walked among the wreckage tending them and pouring champagne into their wounds as an antiseptic.[5]

Three days later, thirty-four incendiaries fell on The London Hospital, but fortunately all were quickly extinguished before they could cause much damage. Rose, writing to her aunt in Wales, explained how the hospital coped with air raids:

The most important people are matron and the medical officer in charge. They spend a lot of time reassuring patients and staff and calling up extra people when we need them. They are in touch with fire watchers, hospital porters and engineers. We have extra receiving and resuscitation rooms during a long raid. Separate areas are marked out for the dead and their belongings. When we have time we are supposed to make them look reasonable for identification by relatives. This isn't always possible. Some injuries are too dreadful for words. Our canteen is open all through the night and we have reserve water supplies and electricity. Ward stoves are fuelled by oil. The medical officer makes sure that we take a break after a few hours, he usually has to order us to do this because we don't want to leave our patients. Two days ago a young soldier on leave came to look for his family. Poor sister had to gently tell him they were all dead. His parents, three sisters and a brother. I will never forget the shock on his face, white as snow, drained of all blood. I rushed to find a chair for him. He'd been through Dunkirk and several battles, only to come home to this bomb scarred city and a dead family. He was inconsolable.

Very little could be done to ease the sorrow of grief-stricken relatives. Some were supported by family members, but others were simply left to 'get on with things'. Whether abroad or at home, by this stage, most Britons had lost a family member or friend. Furthermore, there was no time for long periods of mourning. Propaganda assured everyone that 'Britain can take it', and encouraged people to bounce back from adversity as quickly as possible:

> Britain is guarding the frontiers of freedom and as the familiar searchlights scan the sky the greatest civilian army ever assembled gets ready for the night. Bombing has had a terrific effect on the people – a surging spirit of courage such as the world has never seen before. London may be hurt in the night but the sign of a great fighter in the ring is – can he get up after a fall? Londoners do this every day and bombs cannot kill the unconquerable spirit of Londoners.[6]

However, after months of bombing, Londoners were heartily sick of 'taking it' and there were growing calls to start 'giving it back'. Consequently, the Ministry of Information eventually shelved 'Britain can take it' films because they were deemed to be too defeatist and undermined morale. London hospital administrators attempted to shore up staff morale by introducing concerts, dances, debates and lectures. Often these gatherings brought people together from various hospital departments, a policy which fostered cohesion and a sense of belonging.

Medical officers continually stressed the importance of staff loyalty to each individual hospital, also emphasising that efficient organisation of staff was just as crucial to the successful running of a wartime hospital as it was to a battalion in the field of battle.

Moreover, prolonged raids continued to wreak havoc and destruction throughout March, April and May. During a raid which took place on 11 March, a large bomb fell on Whitechapel station. The fallout from the explosion shattered the windows of The London, just as seventy-six casualties were being admitted from bombs which had fallen to the east of the hospital. Four nurses injured by a bomb landing on the London Chest Hospital in Victoria Park were also admitted to The London. On 16 April, a surgeon at The London, named Norman Oatley, was slightly injured as he tended bomb victims, and on 19 April a heavy raid destroyed much of Peter's Hospital in Vallance Road. An auxiliary fire station was obliterated in the same raid, killing six firemen, two telephonists and two young boys who had been working as messenger runners. Mrs Peters, mother of three evacuated children and one of the dead telephonists, had been working at the fire station for two years. The other dead telephonist was 21-year-old Miss Hilda Dupree; she was due to marry her fireman fiancé in two weeks.

On 10 May, The London Hospital was hit yet again. All essential services were out of action, windows smashed to smithereens and doors blown off their hinges. Nevertheless, The London still managed to admit the injured, and patients from nearby Poplar Hospital, which had sustained severe damage. Further down the road a bomb dropped on Mann's brewery, killing twenty-five of their horses. Several other horses, frightened and loose, stampeded out of control. It took over an hour for hospital porters to steer the horses into the hospital car park and tie them securely to wooden posts. During the same night, Westminster Abbey, the Houses of Parliament and the British Museum were damaged. There were also some lucky escapes. An ambulance driver named Mr Wells was fire-watching outside his house when a bomb crashed on top of it. He knew his 2-year-old son Kenneth was inside, asleep on the first floor, and he dug frantically to find him. When he found Kenneth, safe and unharmed, he was under his bed, which had been turned upside down. The first thing Kenneth said to his father was: 'Woo Woo turned my bed over.' Woo Woo was the family dog.

During this heavy raid five hospitals were bombed, and press reports were full of admiration for hospital staff, particularly the nurses:

> Although it is severely damaged and every window broken the London hospital is carrying on. Several wards were completely wrecked and Saturday night the outpatients were demolished but no one hurt. At another hospital four wards were wrecked and a number of people, including a night sister, a woman dispenser and a roof spotter were killed. A sister had an amazing escape when a bomb fell, and at once began rescuing eighteen men patients who were under the debris. With the help of nurses she saved them all except one. Two men were killed and six injured. Those who escaped had just finished extricating their colleagues when the hospital was hit. Immediately they ran to the hospital and helped the nurses in the rescue work.[7]

A few days later, another nurse heroine was in the news:

> Lying in a telephone kiosk in Victoria hospital for children London, during a recent raid was the only patient, four month old Victor Bailey. All the other children had been evacuated. Every time a bomb screamed down a nurse threw herself over the baby to shield him from flying glass fragments. Both escaped unharmed. When a bomb blew in the ward shelter protection the nurse Sister Hicks had picked up the baby and taken him to the phone box in the entrance hall. 'Her presence of mind undoubtedly saved him,' said the hospital secretary yesterday. 'For there was nowhere else in the hospital she could have gone.'[8]

Following these latest raids, Londoners began to seriously question and doubt the safety of their hospitals. In response to these fears, the Minister of Health issued a statement:

Although they have been damaged by bombs hospitals are not unsafe places during air raids and people do not run a special risk by entering them. In four hundred hospitals and institutions of all kinds in Greater London, casualties among patients totalled only four hundred and thirty, of whom two hundred and thirty five were killed and one hundred and ninety five injured, the majority only slightly. Because of the very elaborate precautions we have taken to meet conditions of heavy raiding, the risk is less than outside hospitals.[9]

This speech did much to reassure most Londoners. However, when Lord Horder conducted a survey of conditions in Underground shelters, he discovered that some parents were keeping their children underground for up to three weeks at a time. Deprived of sunshine and fresh air, these same children were in danger of developing rickets and were more likely to succumb to all manner of diseases. They also slipped through the net of medical screening and immunisation programmes. Chief Medical Officer of Health Sir William Jameson, concerned about this trend, issued 'golden rules' for building up reserves of health:

1 Go out in the fresh air as much as possible. Grab all the sunshine you can, and get it direct, not through windows.
2 Get out of the frame of mind of always associating meat and veg as one dish.
3 We are going to be more and more dependent on our own home-grown vegetables. Eat as many as possible and eat the national wheat-meal loaf, which is endorsed by the whole medical opinion of this country.
4 Get immunised against Diphtheria.[10]

Several press articles endorsed these guidelines and hammered home the sunshine and fresh air message. They also highlighted the positive effects of rationing and exercise. Consequently, as spring gave way to summer, in spite of the stressful, terrifying horrors of bombing, hospital records revealed that Britons were beginning to get slimmer, fitter and healthier.

Notes

1 Curnock, G.C., *Hospitals Under Fire* (1941), p. 71.
2 *Ibid.*, p. 56.
3 *Ibid.*, p. 57.
4 *Ibid.*, p. 59–60.
5 'Dance hall bombing', *Daily Mirror*, 11 March 1941.
6 *London can take it*, Ministry of Information propaganda film 1940.
7 *Daily Mirror*, 12 May 1941.
8 *Ibid.*, 17 May 1941.
9 Minister of Health, speaking in the House of Commons, 30 April 1941. The figures quoted, therefore, do not include the dead and wounded for May 1941.
10 Ministry of Health Information Circular, May 1941.

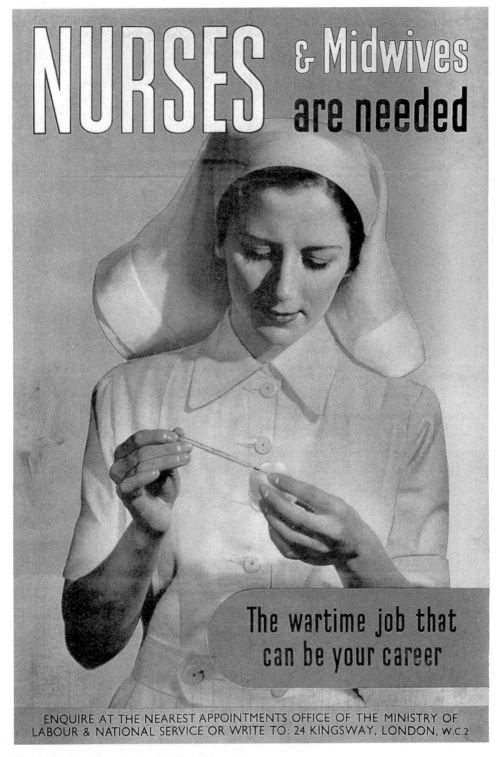

Nurse recruitment poster. (Wellcome Collection)

St Thomas' training centre, pre-war. (Wellcome Collection)

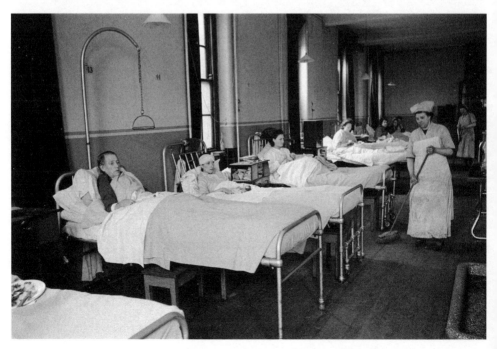

8 February 1945. Casualties in the hospital after a V-2 rocket incident at Bethnal Green. (Mirrorpix)

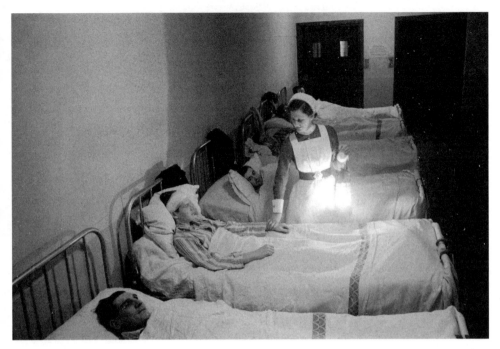

24 December 1940. Christmas Eve at Westminster Hospital. (Mirrorpix)

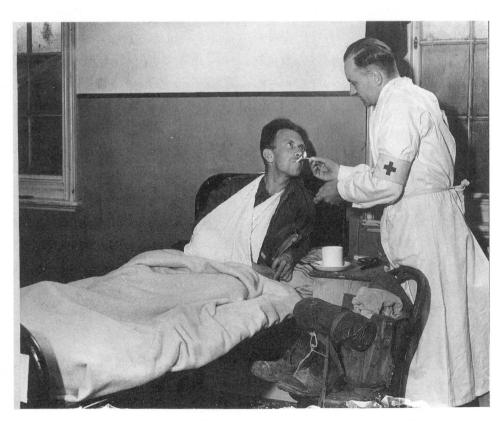

June 1944. A wounded soldier getting a light from a nurse in a hospital near London. (Mirrorpix)

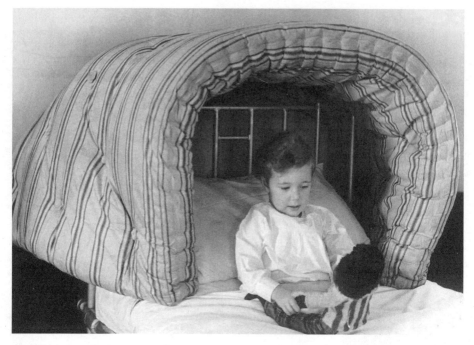

Derek Boosey in his 'lucky horseshoe' in the children's ward of Grove Road Hospital in Tooting, where a bomb had struck. (Mirrorpix)

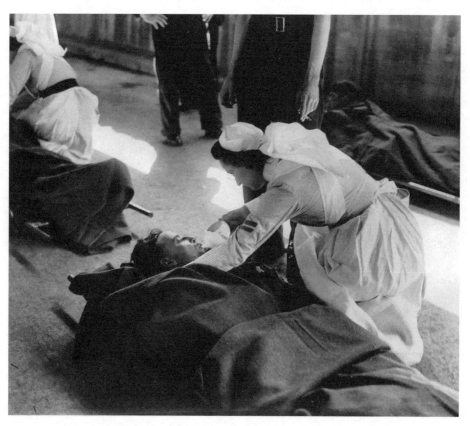

A wounded British soldier evacuated from Europe arrives at a London hospital. (Mirrorpix)

March 1942. Volunteers for the mustard gas tests at the London Homeopathic Hospital. (Mirrorpix)

William Houston making artificial legs at Roehampton Hospital, London. (Mirrorpix)

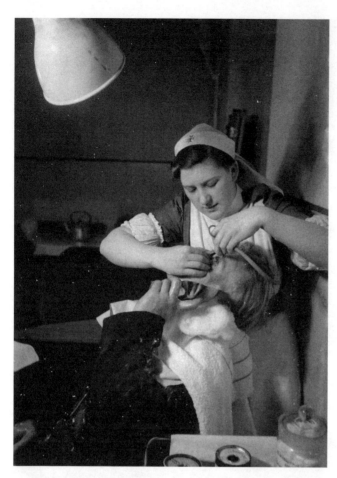

March 1941. A nurse at Westminster Hospital administering first aid during the Blitz. (Mirrorpix)

1 March 1941. Civil Defence workers receiving treatment at Westminster Hospital Aid Post. (Mirrorpix)

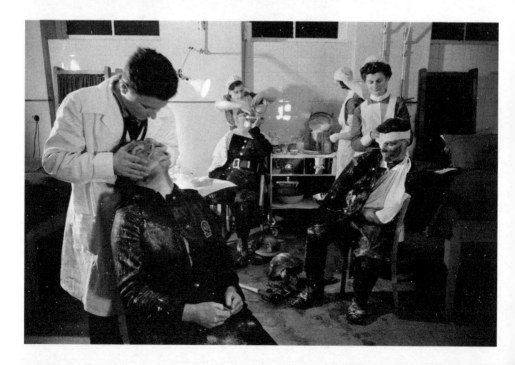

9 April 1941. Bomb damage to The London Hospital. (Mirrorpix)

2 March 1941. Bomb damage at the London Chest Hospital, Bethnal Green. (Mirrorpix)

April 1944. Nurses finding salvageable equipment in the wreckage of a London hospital. (Mirrorpix)

Firemen search through the remains of a London hospital after an air raid by German bombers. (Mirrorpix)

8 February 1945. Casualties outside Bethnal Green Hospital after a V-2 rocket incident. (Mirrorpix)

August 1940. Girls and a nurse holding a baby looking out through the smashed window of a bomb–damaged maternity unit in a London hospital. (Mirrorpix)

10

MEDICAL ADVANCES

Towards the end of May, bombing raids on London began to lessen in frequency and intensity, primarily because Hitler diverted some German aircraft to assist the shambolic Italians in their efforts to conquer Greece. Then, on 22 June, despite the earlier non-aggression pact he had signed with Stalin, Hitler chose to invade the Soviet Union. However, the need for Germany to intervene in Greece had seriously delayed this invasion. Code-named Operation Barbarossa, it signalled the beginning of the end for the German forces, since later in the year they struggled to cope with the severe Russian winter. British forces had withdrawn from Crete and were mounting a strong counteroffensive against German troops in North Africa. But the success of desert warfare was largely dependent on sea warfare, because most of the supplies to British troops in this area were shipped across the Mediterranean. Therefore, battles for the control of the Mediterranean also intensified.

On the Home Front, advances in medical care speeded up patient recovery times and mobile X-ray units improved diagnosis rates, especially in the armed forces. As Monica Baly recalled: 'You had a pressure to get people back to duty, particularly in the Air Force where you were dealing with people like pilots who were very valuable and precious. You had to get them back into the air as quickly as possible.'[1]

The rapid speed at which aeroplanes on fire hurtled to the ground produced what became known as 'airman's burns'. These burns caused deep penetration and destruction of body tissue. They were initially treated with sulphonamide powder and Vaseline gauze, or tannic acid, until a pioneering plastic surgeon named Archibald McIndoe devised new treatments. Tulle gras dressings were introduced and affected limbs were suspended in saline bags to aid healing. McIndoe established his 'Guinea Pig' unit at Queen Victoria Hospital in East Grinstead, where he concentrated on the psychological and physical well-being of his patients. Furthermore, the previously high mortality rate from facial-maxillary injuries was reduced dramatically as highly mobile units treated facial wounds as a matter of urgency. In cases where men's faces had been burned away, surgeons operated in stages:

> Over the course of weeks flesh and skin was replaced and noses swung down in flaps from foreheads, even being so careful as to include a tiny edge of the hair bearing skin where it would normally meet the forehead. This was turned around into this new nose to be tucked inside the nostril so that there were hairs in the nostril.[2]

Most medical innovations originated within military realms, and were subsequently adopted in fits and starts by civilian medical teams. The same was true of nursing care. Working in various theatres of war, military nurses, for example, discovered:

> A shortage of supplies and difficult working conditions meant that you had to make do and improvise. Nurses found themselves very good at improvising, and also discovered that a lot of things that had been done by rote for years, and that they had been trained to do, were no longer necessary. You found, in fact, that when the bombs were falling you could get patients out of bed immediately after an operation and they didn't die. You could operate on patients without

them being starved for twenty four hours and it didn't matter much. It was cook book nursing to some extent and we followed the recipe. We found, as well, that we could make other recipes for ourselves.[3]

Civilian nurses, in contrast, were stuck with outdated routines, and an overload of domestic duties. During the summer months, probationers were also expected to revise for their examinations. Rose and her friends were amongst the many trying to study at the end of each shift. They had taken a few weeks to recover from the restaurant bombing but Rose, Florence and Grace had managed to regain their equilibrium. Gladys, however, still had nightmares about the event:

> I am fearful of crowded places now. It is ridiculous when you think of how random bombing is. When I go to sleep I dream that I am one of the girls sitting next to the dance floor, and then … everything goes black. I wake up in a cold sweat.
>
> I try to study but my mind keeps wandering back to that dreadful night. There is a Canadian man on our ward called Frank, he was caught up in another dance hall bombing and has a fractured femur. His body is recovering well but his mind is dogged with shadows. I thought the bombing was making him anxious, but he told me recently that his wife is back in Canada and he's been receiving anonymous letters about her behaviour. The letters claim that a man is visiting his wife every week – sometimes staying overnight. Frank is eaten up with worry and despair. I told him there could be any number of explanations for such visits, but he doesn't really listen. Whoever is writing such letters must be very malicious. Frank is such a nice young man, very polite, being so very far from home is very hard for him. It doesn't help matters to be bed bound – too much time on his hands to dwell on things.

Hockey, who, amongst other things, was researching the impact of visiting times on patient welfare, was inclined to agree with Gladys. According to Hockey, long periods of inactivity, an absence of visitors and a lack of diversions led to unhealthy introspection. Meanwhile Rose, who had bounced back to her cheerful self after her birthday evening with remarkable speed, was again preoccupied with her appearance. Slightly mollified by a belated birthday card and a hand-carved wooden 'key of the door' from Harold, she returned to her favourite hobby, that of emulating Hollywood film stars. When teased by her friends for her obsession with glamour, Rose would simply tell them that glamour encouraged men to fight harder and was good for the war effort. Government officials and the national press seemed to support this view, and Rose was not alone in taking this stand. In an article entitled 'Lipstick: Nurses win the day' the press gleefully reported on the decision of the British Red Cross Society to lift the bans on make-up and smoking in uniform.

The relaxations follow an unexpectedly poor response to the society's new drive for more full-time voluntary workers. There were conditions, still, which had to be observed by nurses. Make-up must not be too conspicuous and varnished nails still came under the society's list of don'ts. Nurses in uniform could now smoke indoors when not on hospital duty, and they would be permitted an after lunch cigarette in restaurants, cafes and cinemas. But a strict ban still existed on smoking in uniform in the street. An official of the society said that 'nurses have told us they feel conspicuous without some sort of make-up'. The new rules allowed a certain amount of lipstick powder and other make-up. The battle over make-up had raged for years. Mrs C.B. Fellowes, VAD Assistant Commandant, resigned her post at Rushbrook Hall, Suffolk, a month earlier because she was forbidden to wear make-up.[4]

Government officials at the Ministry of Labour held the view that although women were required in greater numbers to undertake men's work, they should also retain their femininity. This view was shared by senior military personnel, on the premise that attractive women shored up male morale. Therefore, when make-up was in short supply, women in the Auxiliary Territorial Service were encouraged to get together in groups according to skin colour shades, in order to share their make-up. For the most part, however, senior nurses were disparaging about make-up, or indeed any other form of adornment, but admitted:

'How women choose to disfigure themselves off duty is beyond any power of intervention.'[5]

Yet government propaganda continued to glamorise nurses and their work in an effort to entice young girls into the profession. Recruitment posters pictured nurses in full make-up, including bright red lipstick. Even advertisements for soap and beauty products used nurses as their ideal: 'The nursing profession teaches the importance of scrupulous cleanliness. It is the only way to skin health and skin beauty. That is why a daily bath with the rich, velvety, olive oil lather of Palmolive will cleanse, soothe and beautify – keep your school girl complexion all over.'[6]

However, all this trivial nonsense diverted attention away from the more urgent issues confronting the profession such as poor pay, dreadful hours and monastic living conditions. As Monica Baly recalled: 'The problem of nurse status did loom large and nurses in the civilian field did feel lowly regarded.'[7]

Home helps, lady's maids, companions for the elderly and others in domestic service often used the term 'nurse' to advertise their services, a practice which was misleading for the general public and derogatory to registered nurses. Within the armed forces the indomitable matron-in-chief, Dame Katherine Jones, took matters into her own hands. By assimilating military nurse hierarchy to the army pattern and moving registered nurses to front-line positions, Dame Katherine ensured that her registered nurses were afforded commissioned officer status in 1941. This event was also significant to civilian registered nurses, since they now had a point of reference for their own status. As the militarising matron-in-chief explained to the civilian Association of Hospital Matrons:

> To me, officer rank with all its symbols, its privileges, its duties and its traditions, is a living reality. It means responsibility and heard earned privilege reflecting professional and military achievement. Can you therefore be surprised that conferment of commissioned rank on the Queen Alexandra's Imperial Military Nursing Service was the most significant day of my working life? To me it was the recognition of

the status which a State Registered Nurse should enjoy in relation to auxiliary personnel.

It was inevitable therefore that the commissioning of the Q.A.I.M.N.S. and the T.A.N.S. – and I want you to understand this as the imposition of the military rank pattern on the nursing profession – seemed to me to be an event of the first importance. By superimposing this rank pattern of the Army on one particular section of the nursing profession, it seemed possible, not merely to confer status but to provide a framework which would hold that status in place.[8]

Senior civilian nurses did take on board a superficial notion of officer status, but most failed dismally to incorporate the leadership aspects which were required of the military officer class. Thus, civilian nurses were left to work with an outdated military model of nursing, whilst military nurses forged ahead with new techniques and innovative medical treatments. Furthermore, by virtue of her officer status the military nurse had some political leverage within the military framework, whereas the civilian nurse had no such leverage. In charge of the Civil Nursing Reserve, the Ministry of Health was the largest employer of nurses, but repeatedly favoured quantity over quality despite advice from nurses at Whitehall. The government was also subsidising voluntary hospitals, and medical officers increasingly called for the state to take over the running of all hospitals on a permanent basis.

Some voluntary hospitals did rather well from donations. The Hospital Savings Association also distributed £75,000 to London voluntary hospitals. In the financial year 1940–41, The London Hospital received £22,710 (interim payment) – £4,452; Guy's Hospital, £11,772 – £2,294; St Bartholomew's Hospital, £12,365 – £2,364; Middlesex Hospital, £10,394 – £2,205; St Thomas' Hospital, £9,575 – £1,875; King's College Hospital, £7,700 – £1,498.[9]

Nevertheless, voluntary hospitals across the country still relied heavily on fundraising activities to continue their work. On 21 October 1941, demands for a state takeover of these institutions received cross-party support in the House of Commons. Dr Edith Summerskill, Labour MP for West Fulham, asked the House:

> Is there anything ennobling in our large teaching hospitals having to send out their students and nurses to make clowns of themselves in the street, and for their secretaries to have to sit and think how to make money out of bridge parties, dances and concerts to get more money out of the public? These hospitals because they have insufficient funds are economising at the expense of their patients. It had been said that the honorary staffs of these hospitals gave their services without hope of reward. The fact is, that the best way of creating a remunerative private practice is to be appointed to the staff of a voluntary hospital. That is why there is such competition to get onto the staffs.[10]

A handful of MPs argued that a state-run health service, though desirable, might prove to be inefficient. There was, however, widespread approval amongst the younger generation of medical students. Independent Conservative MP for Cambridge University, Dr A.V. Hill, recounted some information obtained from a medical student based at St Bartholomew's Hospital, who claimed that it had been impossible to hold a debate on the issue of a state medical service because no one could be found to oppose the suggestion. Dr Hill stated emphatically: 'I cannot believe that a state service is necessarily inefficient – the Royal Navy is not inefficient.'[11]

MPs also discussed the state of public health. According to the Minister of Health, the maternal mortality rate was down on the previous year, as was the tuberculosis mortality rate. For the first quarter of 1941, there was a reduction of 7 per cent in the numbers of tuberculosis cases compared with the first quarter of 1940. This downward trend was continuing, but there were still ninety-eight deaths per week from the disease. However, since people were huddled together night after night in Underground and other public shelters, the rate of infectious diseases had soared. For instance, whooping cough had claimed 678 lives in 1940, compared to 2,383 lives in 1941. The number of deaths from measles had also risen from 857 cases in 1940 to 1,145 cases in 1941. In the same year there were 50,000 recorded cases of diphtheria and the disease had claimed the lives of 2,641 children in England and Wales. Ministry of Health policy had aimed to immunise 75 per cent of children before the end of 1941, but fell severely short of this target by only immunising 33 per cent. This shortfall was mainly due to the reluctance of local health authorities to comply with Whitehall directives, and the influence of an aggressive anti-vaccination league.[12]

Furthermore, just as nurses working in sanatoriums often caught tuberculosis, nurses working with children frequently succumbed to infectious diseases. Senior nurses, meanwhile, were beginning to suffer from the effects of stress, as they tried to administer their dislocated staff. Dr Clark-Kennedy, who was trying to keep the London medical school together, reported that there was considerable friction amongst some matrons:

> The nursing school had suffered even more than the medical school from dispersal at the beginning of the war, and from chaos of the blitz. It has not been easy to maintain London hospital standards in 'other peoples' hospitals. The nursing school has been disrupted by war. Miss Reynolds was matron of sector one and shared responsibilities for the training of London hospital nurses with Miss Burgess, acting matron at the London, and Miss Walker who was matron of sector two. The situation was, in fact, awkward and only resolved by the resignation of Miss Reynolds. This left the House Committee free to act. Miss Alexander an 'old Londoner' was offered the matron-ship and accepted it on the understanding that she became matron of both sectors and ran them from The London, in this way gaining control of the nursing at all hospitals where London nurses were working. The new matron spent as much time travelling round her far flung nursing school as I did in trying to keep my scattered medical school together.[13]

A growing shortage of male staff enabled the matron of The London to take over the running of operating theatres for the first time, and

Miss Ida Latham was appointed superintendent of theatre staff. This was a significant innovation, which signalled the expansion of professional nursing. Nevertheless, not everything went according to plan. Since the government had swamped the profession with untrained young girls, there were numerous incidences of dangerous or neglectful nursing practice. In fact, such girls were often a liability. One young girl, when counting the swabs at an orthopaedic operation, said that the number was correct even though she knew she had recounted and there was one missing. Later, she said she did this for 'peace and happiness' as the surgeon was getting irritable.[14]

Yet, whilst registered nurses were doing everything in their power to protect their status, the average probationer seemed oblivious to such political wrangling. Probationer diaries and letters were focussed on everyday matters, concerns for their patients, current romances, workloads and examinations. Flo, for instance, was full of dread following her viva and reported in her notebook:

> I was asked about the importance of personal hygiene and answered the best I could. My examiner had a face like stone and gave no indication of whether she approved or disapproved of my ramblings. Our tutor room was completely empty and looked odd without the usual furniture. The next question was about the dietary requirements of abdominals, and I blurted out as much as I knew about soft bland food. I thought it was all over and then she enquired whether or not I knew how to treat shock. This was something I thought I could talk about forever, because we'd nursed so many shocked bomb victims in recent months. But her face looked so stern and I found myself bumbling almost incoherently. I knew the answer but nerves got the better of me and I am sure I will have to re-sit in a few months.

Grace approached her examinations as she did everything else, sensibly, quietly and without fuss or drama. Even her finals were a source of irritation rather than anxious trepidation. Writing of them in her diary: 'I am so glad they are out of the way now. They are such a nuisance and revision takes up so much time. Nursing is a fascinating job, but constantly having to prove your worth is very tiresome!'

Rose rarely mentioned examinations in her letters or diaries, merely stating that she had to revise over and over again because her memory was poor. Gladys, meanwhile, was yet again full of self-doubt, and seriously considering the prospect of leaving the profession, something she did on at least a weekly basis, although her friends frequently remarked on the fact that she also spent a lot of time worrying about her patients and was instinctively in tune with most of them. Frank, her Canadian patient, for example, seemed to Gladys to be distant and despairing when he was eventually discharged:

> He has a black cloud hovering over him. When he smiles his smile doesn't reach his eyes. They are dull and listless, full of pain and sadness. I'm sure he should not be leaving our care quite so soon. There is no energy about him. No enthusiasm for life. His friends are chivvying him along but I worry for his future.

Gladys was right to be concerned. Two weeks after his discharge, Frank took his own life. Overwhelmed by the thought that his wife was being unfaithful, he hanged himself in a warehouse. Investigations subsequently made by senior military personnel revealed that Frank's wife was indeed being visited once a week by a man. The man turned out to be her father, who was calling by her house to check on her well-being and to ask if she needed anything. Frank had taken his life needlessly, all because of the malicious actions of an interfering neighbour. National press articles used Frank's demise to highlight the dangers of believing information received by means of anonymous communications, arguing that there were always those who sought to destroy morale and undermine the war effort. Soldiers who were a long way from home were particularly vulnerable to poison pen letters, and the press stated that it was up to the British people to protect them from troublemakers and imbue them with courage. This was easier said than done, and Gladys felt as though she had personally failed Frank.

She had known of his deep despair and had been unable to alleviate his mental suffering. Haunted by his demise and persistent self-doubt, she confided to her diary:

> I am not really any good to anyone as a nurse. I try my hardest but it is never enough. At the end of my shift I always think that I could have done more. I wish I had more time to listen to patients, more time to give them attention. Everything is done in a rush and the shortage of domestics mean that we now do most of the cleaning too. How many other Franks are there? What could we have been done to help him? I feel so utterly useless. I do so envy Rose. She seems to float through life with hardly a care. Troubles are like water off a duck's back. She doesn't dwell on the condition of any patient and always has a joke or funny story to lighten the mood. She says I think too much. Perhaps she's right. Sister tutor says I have a tendency to be morose!

However, although Rose appeared to sail through life, her letters to her aunt revealed an underlying anxiety:

> Summer days are truly wonderful but I sometimes wonder how many more there will be. There was a heavy raid at the end of July and it felt like the end of the world. Buildings crashing down once again, shattered bodies jamming our hospital corridors, blood everywhere and people urgently hunting for their loved ones. We need to treasure every moment, every cloudless sky, every warm breeze, the chance to bask in sunshine, to wear flimsy cotton dresses, watch boats along the Thames, hold hands with our sweet-hearts, cuddle the children and stroll through the parks – moments like these can be gone in an instant.

Clearly Rose used humour and flippancy in her working life as a way of masking her own morose tendencies. Whilst she did not dwell unduly on her patients' problems, she was by no means oblivious to them. Within her friendship circle she was viewed as a scatterbrained hedonistic character, preoccupied with film stars, glamour, romance and dancing. Yet she hid a far deeper side to her nature, a side she did not reveal in her diaries or notebooks, and not even in her letters to Harold. Rose only expressed her anxieties and intense observations about life during the Blitz when writing to her aunt.

Concern over patient welfare was not simply the preserve of the nursing and medical profession. Hospital supply records reveal levels of collective anxiety as the strain of providing care for bomb victims on a nightly basis took its toll. Most of this anxiety was caused by shortages of medicines, dressings and intravenous fluids. Blood supplies were also a problem, and American donors responded wholeheartedly to rallying calls for blood. However, there were well-founded concerns over the purity of blood donated in the United States, as Nazi sympathisers frequently sabotaged attempts to send supplies across the Atlantic.

According to the *New York Times*, several attempts had been made to contaminate American blood destined for the battlefields:

> At least two attempts have been made to poison blood donated in New York for British wounded. Captain Charles Skully of the American Red Cross, yesterday revealed to John Walters a New York Correspondent. In one attempt needles were inserted through the rubber caps and aluminium seals of a bottle of blood and poisonous matter injected. This outrage was discovered when the blood was examined before shipment to England. In another hospital everything was ready for taking blood from volunteer donors when all instruments were found to be contaminated with poison.[15]

In terms of finance, donations of material goods and life-saving blood, America had undeniably pinned its flag to the British cause. American politicians, however, including President Franklin D. Roosevelt, were reluctant to be drawn into war. Nevertheless, Winston Churchill, who was a doggedly determined character, was convinced he could persuade Roosevelt of the need for American military aid, later confiding that: 'No lover ever studied the whims of his mistress as I did those of President Roosevelt.'[16]

As summer turned to autumn, Churchill increased his efforts to bring America into the war, and British hospitals prepared for another winter of bombing raids.

Notes

1 *Frontline Females*, vol. 1.
2 *Ibid.*
3 *Ibid.*
4 'Lipstick: nurses win the day', *Daily Mail*, quoted in the *British Journal of Nursing*, March 1941.
5 *British Journal of Nursing*, March 1941.
6 *Daily Mirror*, 17 July 1942.
7 Oral History interview with Dr Monica Baly, conducted 7 June 1994.
8 National Archive: War Office 222/178.
9 *British Journal of Nursing*, March 1941, p. 43.
10 Hansard, House of Commons Parliamentary Debates 5th series, 21 October 1941.
11 *Ibid.*
12 For a more in-depth examination of childhood epidemics during the Second World War, please see Starns, P., *Blitz Families: the Children who Stayed Behind* (2012).
13 Clark-Kennedy, A.E., *London Pride* (1979), p. 225.
14 Matron's register, Royal London Hospital.
15 *New York Times*, 11 March 1941.
16 Meacham, J., *Franklin and Winston* (2003), p. 130.

NURSING IN CRISIS

In November 1941, the British 8th Army began an offensive in Libya. The Russians, meanwhile, recaptured Rostov. Then, on 7 December, Japanese forces launched an attack on Pearl Harbor that virtually destroyed America's Pacific fleet. The following day, Britain and America declared war on Japan, and on 10 and 11 December America declared war on Germany and Italy. Moreover, after some intense political wrangling, Churchill managed to convince Roosevelt that the Allies needed to concentrate their efforts on winning the war in Europe before tackling the war in the Far East.

On the Home Front, Londoners were preparing for Christmas imbued with a new optimism. Tinsel, baubles and Christmas trees topped with white crepe-paper angels were carried down to Underground shelters. The Anglo-American Relief Organization supplied a mountain of toys and sweets for the children, and Christmas parties were held across the city. Carol concerts accompanied by banjos, guitars, ukuleles and accordions were enthusiastically attended, and there was a growing recognition that victory over Germany was only a matter of time. On New Year's Day 1942, the United Nations Declaration was signed by twenty-six nations, which pledged the military and economic support of the signatories against Germany and Italy.[1]

With victory almost in sight, Ministry of Health officials began to look to the possibility of future reconstruction, and once more, there were public calls for a state-run health system. Dr Clark-Kennedy recalled the scenario at The London at this time:

Early in 1942, the Ministry thought it safe to open more beds and allowed the London to increase its complement to 446 while still maintaining 336 beds at Brentwood. Many honorary staff out in the sectors returned to work in the hospital or at Brentwood. Matron too, brought back more nurses. These changes were soon reflected in the work done. In 1941, 6,000 patients were admitted to the London. In 1942 this figure rose to 8,000 and out-patient attendance from 42,000 to over 56,000. These statistics did not include emergency medical scheme hospitals at Chase Farm in Hertfordshire and Warley Woods in Essex, and two maternity homes in Hertfordshire and Essex. The London, although still scattered was, in fact, almost twice as large as any other hospital at this time. It was doing more than twice their amount of work. Other steps in reconstruction were also considered safe.

The school of physical medicine was brought back from Northampton; the radium and radon laboratory from Bedfordshire, and certain innovations were permitted. Radiotherapy was separated from radio diagnosis and a department of the former set up under the Cancer Act of 1939 to provide for East Anglia. A school of radiotherapy was started, and an almoners department to supplement the work of the Samaritan Society. Reginald Watson Jones was invited from Liverpool to get an orthopaedic and accident department under way. But the problem of the chronic sick remained. It was becoming increasingly clear that some unified hospital system was needed. Municipal hospitals were dangerously overcrowded and voluntary hospitals were relatively empty – refusing to have beds blocked by the chronic sick.[2]

Despite the reconstruction, in medical schools there were shortages associated with medical teaching aids at this time, especially human skeletons for anatomy lessons. Before the war, hundreds of such skeletons were imported from Germany for use in British hospitals and universities, but once hostilities began these institutions could only obtain a limited supply from India. Furthermore, although the Ministry of Health encouraged hospitals to increase their bed capacity, nurses were leaving their hospitals in droves. Newspapers reported on staffing problems yet again:

> Our nurses are working long hours. Many of them fill a ninety six hour fortnight and under a new Treasury ruling they are allowed only a fourteen day leave. There is a shortage of hospital servants and the matron of a London hospital told me that she had to ask her trained nurses to do a thousand and one jobs outside their own nursing work.[3]

An eminent physician, Dr F.B. Julian, addressed nursing associations in an attempt to get senior nurses to release their stranglehold on probationers:

> People expect nurses to be run off their feet for a salary which would make a kitchen maid sniff contemptuously. Liberties are taken with nurses' off-duty time which no mistress would dare take with their maids. Hours are far too long. In some hospitals there is an almost monastic conception of a nurses' calling. Girls will not rush into the profession while such conditions prevail.[4]

Nursing shortages were not simply confined to hospitals. District nurses were leaving because petrol restrictions were making their work impossible. Petrol rationing did not allow for emergency calls, only routine visits. Moreover, nurses working within the prison service made a deputation to Whitehall to complain about the fact that they were forced to live in cells:

> At one gaol, the nurses' living quarters are converted cells on a landing reserved for women with venereal disease and scabies. These nurses live

all the time in a prison environment and when they get out, they are short leave for they have to be back in gaol before the gates are locked. They are appealing for quarters outside prisons and commissioners are sympathetic, but the Ministry of Works and Buildings say no new construction can be put up in war time. So in the meantime, these trained nurses have to live in cells, in gaol with criminals, and attend to fascists who are having a comfortable time. No wonder there is a shortage of prison nurses.[5]

There were shortages in midwifery too, and women generally had an axe to grind with regard to their treatment. On 9 September, representations from fifty-two women's associations invaded the House of Commons to raise the issue of unfair compensation payments for war injuries. They put their case before Deputy Prime Minister Clement Attlee:

Men cheered their women folk as they spoke, 'I shop, I cook and look after my children. I think I am worth a good wage,' said housewife Sheila Jones of Harrow, who had left her four children (all under ten) with a neighbour while she joined the deputation. 'I am a useful wife to my husband' she added. 'Therefore, I think I am a good servant to the government. Dealing with rationing and feeding the future generation is my job, yet if I am injured by a bomb I receive seven shillings a week less than a man who doesn't work at all.'[6]

Across the country, women were rallying to demand better wages, work conditions and family allowances. Even members of the rather timid Royal College of Nursing were writing to the Minister of Home Security to demand that nurses be relieved of fire-watching duties, on the grounds that they were needed to nurse the injured. But despite the wartime reliance on women, very little was done at this stage to address their demands. It was not so easy for government officials to ignore the nursing crisis, however, and they spent over £166,000 on recruitment propaganda. This included the production of a propaganda film, designed to appeal to potential recruits, entitled *The Lamp Still Burns*. Starring

Stewart Granger and Rosamund John, the film emphasised the military roots of British nursing, the heroic and vocational calling of nurses, and the profession's valuable contribution to the war effort. Matron Clare Alexander of The London was adviser to the film production company and the script was written with the help of senior nurses at Whitehall. Amidst the romantic drama, the film contained a stern message to hospital matrons – they needed to relax their attitudes towards nurse discipline or risk the prospect of having no nurses to discipline! As the following extracts from the film demonstrate:

> Becoming a nurse is rather like joining the army, only the hospital is always at war against disease and accident. It's like training to be a commando. There simply isn't room for anyone who can't take it. And when you're in uniform my girl, everyone expects everything of you. And in order to give them what they expect, like any soldier, you have to be ready for any sacrifice.[7]

The heroine of the film, Rosamund John, who unsurprisingly falls in love with Stewart Granger, frequently incurs the wrath of matron over some petty misdemeanour. Towards the end of the film, she launches into an impassioned verbal attack on the whole system of nurse training. Criticism of hospital matrons is only thinly disguised as the heroine implores her matron to allow her to continue her career:

> I am prepared to give up my personal freedom and live penned in by petty restrictions. I am even prepared to denounce my rights as a woman to a home and children of my own, because the demands of this profession leave no time for any personal life. I am prepared to submit to all this because I count it a privilege to be allowed to devote my life to nursing. That's why I am grateful to you for giving me the opportunity to state my case, and why I beg you to let me stay on here no matter what the conditions. But are those conditions inevitable? They are not merely the result of wartime measures because it has always been like this, and there has always been a shortage of nurses.

I don't believe they're inevitable and, because I care so much I urge you to agitate for their improvement. I implore you: start a reform. Because if you do, hospitals need never be understaffed again.[8]

Most matrons, however, ignored the core message of the film. They argued that strict discipline was both necessary and character-forming. They also claimed that, once they were married, nurses were required to resign, because the nature of nursing work made it impossible for a woman to combine the role of wife and nurse. Although, in this respect, some matrons were prepared to make exceptions to meet the exigencies of war. The Ministry of Health, guided by Whitehall nurses, belatedly realised that propaganda alone was not likely to resolve nursing issues. In desperation, a committee chaired by Lord Rushcliffe was established to investigate nursing problems and propose solutions.

In the meantime, hospitals continued to struggle, not only with staff shortages but also with food shortages. In London, there were approximately 80,000 staff and patients to support, and by the autumn of 1942 London hospitals were already cultivating 6,000 acres of mixed farmland. A London County Council official stated:

Our aim is to have sufficient acres under cultivation to provide ourselves with as much as possible of the necessities we require. We grow every kind of vegetable, run poultry farms, and have sheep and cows. We also grow grain and fruit. Three hundred and fifty full time labourers and thirty one members of the women's land army are working for the London County Council. Throughout the season batches of school children will supplement their work.[9]

The make-do-and-mend and grow-your-own message was adopted throughout the country. Moreover, despite the long working hours, nurses still managed to enjoy some social relaxation. Rose, Gladys, Grace and Flo were able to organise a get-together in a tea room about once a month, usually an afternoon snatched between split shifts, and could often be found making plans for the future. Rose had become engaged to Harold during his most recent leave and was waxing lyrical about their romance. She wore her diamond and emerald engagement ring on a chain around her neck, because nurses were not allowed to wear jewellery when wearing uniform. Rose, not put off by such a rule, discreetly tucked her ring-bearing chain inside her dress where nobody could see it. She loved nothing more than to retrieve the ring, which had been worn by Harold's grandmother, from its secret hiding place to flaunt it in front of her friends. Gladys quite truthfully declared that she was not interested in romance. Grace claimed that she was too busy organising Girl-Guiding Blitz cookery courses in her spare time to even contemplate the subject. Flo calmly asserted with some feeling that she was far too tired for such diversions, but offered to help make Rose's wedding outfit when required. In fact, Flo felt somewhat ill at ease, because her own romance with Archie had fizzled out. Her mother had shaken her head wisely and said, 'Whatever will be will be', which Flo thought was a distinctly unhelpful remark. Undeterred by her friends' lukewarm response to matters of the heart, Rose tried in vain to convince her friends that love was vitally important. With some relish, she brandished an old newspaper article which backed up her claim. In an article entitled 'Love keeps you fit', newspapers declared:

Love is the most potent of all positive emotions – such as happiness, peace, contentment, hope, as opposed to ill temper, spite, hatred and all the other negative emotions.

It is a scientific fact that the negative emotions generate a poison in the blood so that it really is possible to be physically ill with anger, or spite or jealousy or fear. But love casts out fear, doubt, pessimism, discontent and literally rids the system of poison. That is why a hitherto pale and wan looking girl who has little interest in life takes on a sudden radiance when she finds love. Her cheeks become pink, her eyes brighter. She is physically better because her emotions are happier. And note this. It isn't the fact of being loved that counts but the being able to love! It is what you feel and not what other people feel about you that counts.

A girl never looks miserable and thwarted and left out in the cold if she has room in her heart for those about her. That is why so many women who at present are living in the midst of services or as civil defence workers keep well. Love is a great shock absorber, and the love of humanity is one of the best nerve tonics ever devised. Lose the thought of self in love and service – and so keep fit.[10]

Rose's friends burst into spontaneous laughter. Gladys jokingly pointed out that she did not believe the research unless it had been conducted by Hockey. Grace dismissed the article as utter rubbish, and Flo wanted to know why the article was only about women in love. If it was based on a scientific study, then why didn't it include men? The friends concluded that because young men were not home on leave for long, there was obviously never time to study them. Gladys stated that since it was all about losing self and making sacrifices, the article was simply a propaganda tool aimed at keeping women in their place. Still shocked by the death of Frank, she also asserted that it was foolish to fall in love in such uncertain times. She cited one of her patients as a case in point. A beautiful young bride of three days, who became a widow as she lay in her hospital bed. Her husband had been given a forty-eight-hour pass to get married before returning to his RAF duties. The bride was hit by a car later that evening just after her husband returned to his base. Whilst in hospital recovering from her injuries, news was received that her airman husband had been killed on his first operational flight. The nurses fell silent for a moment. Then Rose and the others expressed their sadness and sympathy for the young couple so cruelly deprived of their future together. A sombre mood engulfed them for a short while. Each exchanged equally sad and dramatic stories of loss. As they rose to leave the tea room, Rose announced that she would pray for Harold every morning before she went onto her ward. Her friends nodded in agreement – they too would pray for their families and friends.

On her return to the nurses' home, Gladys began to read *The London Hospital League Review*. One of the London-trained nurses,

Betty Blanc-Smith, had joined the QAs, and a letter she had written to her parents from the Far East was published in the *Review*:

New Years day! I must simply write you a letter to make up for the lapse of time since my last effort. I sent you a cable the day after war started out here as I knew you would be worried. They assured me at the cable office that it would reach you by Christmas and I do hope that it did so. Goodness knows when you will get this, but I hope it will be before next year! Now there is no clipper service, news will be long in reaching you but don't worry about me – whatever may happen to me cannot but be for the best, and so far I seem to have been so well cared for that I see no reason why protection should suddenly cease, and whatever I go through is all experience and proves one's strength of character and fundamental beliefs. I have no fear for myself and at the present look on life as a great adventure with the unexpected around every corner. I have often felt that this part of the world must be brought into line with the rest of nations, because its God is money. Many people finding themselves now left with nothing are learning life's true values, perhaps for the first time, I think I already know them up to a point, but that has yet to be proved and there is so much to learn. To hold life so cheaply and all one's worldly possessions of no account takes some doing, but it is a lesson many have to learn until experience has taught us it is impossible to forecast reactions. Waiting for the baptism of fire doesn't worry me much except the usual empty feeling at the sound of planes and guns. One sister here has been through France, the Middle East and Greece with amazing experiences and I want to do likewise. At last my existence here seems about to be justified and the year of fun and games preceding this was just the prelude and will be something to be remembered with a tolerant smile.[11]

A note published under the letter in the same *Review* stated that Betty's parents received notification from the War Office on 17 April 1942, informing them that their daughter was posted as missing, presumed to have been captured or killed by the Japanese during the fall of Singapore on 15 February 1942. She was never seen again.

Hitherto, Gladys had envied her military nursing friend Ivy, whose letters were always witty, observant and informative. They told of new nursing techniques and medications, and described her travels to foreign lands. Reading the *Review*, however, jolted Gladys into the reality of military nursing – the prospect of capture and imprisonment. Ivy had noted that one of the reasons registered nurses were afforded officer status in the armed forces was to give them some protection in the event of capture, since officers were usually treated better than those serving in the rank and file.

Other letters from military nurses revealed that it was not only civilian nurses who were facing staff shortages and difficulties in administering care. A sister with the QAIMS Reserve wrote concerning thousands of Polish prisoners of war, who had been released by the Russians in 1942, across the Caspian Sea into Persia:

There must have been thousands of these first arrivals. Practically every disease in medical knowledge could be found among them and particularly deficiency diseases, dysentery, typhus and malaria. Great difficulty was at first experienced in ascertaining the patients' names and this sometimes led to difficult situations, as for example, when a Jewish patient suddenly disappeared and after three days search was discovered to have died and been duly buried in a Catholic grave. The error was rectified to the satisfaction of everyone concerned, including I hope, the Jew. Eventually we found there was an R.A.M.C. orderly who spoke Russian, French and German, and he was made responsible for seeing every new patient and obtaining their name, religion, etc.

In addition to the language difficulty there was of course the caste system among the sepoys and Indian followers. The sweepers would sweep, deal with latrines and bedpans, soiled linen and water; the bhesties would deal with clean water and linen only; the ward boys would deal with food and feeding utensils only; the sepoys would make beds but not touch any soiled linen of dysentery patients.

Neither would they touch a bedpan or help any patient with one no matter how ill the man might be. They could not be relied upon to wash the hands and face of any patient and had an intense dislike of touching dead bodies. The medical officers were fully employed doing the rounds of patients. The R.A.M.C. orderly and sister were the only people available at any time for any job from pitching tents and removing the dead to giving intravenous injections or dressing wounds. My first reaction was to collect materials and spend half an hour cleaning the mouth of a man who was obviously near the end of his life but having much difficulty breathing his last. An hour later a sepoy came to tell me he was dead. That incident snapped something in me and it was suddenly clear what, in broad outline must be done. The individual must be sacrificed; for one trained person to cope with 200 or so in this condition it was obviously impossible to nurse even a fraction as they should be nursed, until the place was properly organized. In each section the same conclusion was reached sooner or later.[12]

With Russia and America as Britain's allies, the nature and pace of war were changing. The loss of Singapore was a bitter blow to the British Government, but by October 1942 significant advances were being made elsewhere, particularly in North Africa. Field Marshal Montgomery and the 8th Army attacked El Alamein, and massive numbers of British and American troops were sent to reinforce the area. In early November, Russian forces staged a strong counteroffensive at Stalingrad. British victories in North Africa indicated that the tide of war had at long last turned in Britain's favour. It was possible, therefore, for government ministers to pursue post-war reconstruction on the Home Front with renewed vigour. A report published by Sir William (later Lord) Beveridge outlined a comprehensive system of social insurance, which advocated a National Health Service, child allowances, economic policies to foster full employment and a National Insurance scheme to prevent abject poverty. His recommendations became the blueprint for a post-war welfare state and encompassed a vision of a new and prosperous future for the British people. Beveridge rightly saw social security as something more than the provision of a minimum cash income. He acknowledged, in his own distinctive language, that apart from 'want', four other 'giants on the road to reconstruction' had to be slain: disease, ignorance, squalor and idleness.[13] The Beveridge Report represented a sincere attempt to provide a resolution to the problems of widespread poverty and disease, and Beveridge managed to sell his recommendations to his somewhat critical colleagues on economic grounds, arguing that they would build a nation fit for industrial pursuit.

With the prospect of a National Health Service looming on the horizon, nursing issues assumed greater significance, and Lord Rushcliffe was urged to speed up his investigations into the profession. Hospitals were already threatened with closure and as winter approached, accompanied by influenza, pneumonia and a worsening of chronic illnesses, it was estimated that 10,000 nurses were urgently needed to meet demands. But living conditions for nurses remained totally out of step with modern life, as Rose explained in a letter to her aunt:

We do not even have the right to use a telephone or receive messages. Very few hospitals make any provision for nurses to have proper communication with the outside world. I don't know any hospital that takes messages for nurses and keeps them safe for when she is off-duty. Anything could happen to our loved ones and we wouldn't know for days. I love my work but most days I cannot be sure of giving my best attention to patients. You know that expression 'sick and tired?' Well I never really understood that phrase until now. I have realised that it is possible to feel so tired that it makes you feel sick also, the food here continues to be bland and I have no appetite. Mother told me I needed a tonic, so I bought Dr Williams' pink pills for nerves. They were 1s/5d for one pack and 3s/5d for a triple pack, so I bought the triple pack. I've been taking them for a fortnight but I can't say I've noticed any difference in my health or energy. Christmas is coming round again and nothing has changed. We still have to put up with lots of stupid rules and petty little notices appear in the nurses' home every week. Reminding us of lights out, the importance of not using too much bread, not using too much water, not using too much heat and so on. Someone pinned up a notice last week reminding us to creep along the corridors and shut doors softly to avoid any undue noise. You'd never think there was a paper shortage! We all have a good moan at toasting time, but we share our funny stories too. It is not all gloom.

However, whilst nurses continued to endure petty restrictions and oppressive living arrangements, they looked forward with hope to Lord Rushcliffe's report. They accurately reasoned that improvements needed to be forthcoming in order to avert a complete breakdown in nursing services. They were also carried along by the general wave of enthusiasm and hope that was sweeping the country, although the national press pointed out that it would take a considerable amount of time and effort to foster goodwill towards all men:

Peace on earth and goodwill towards men? No, we are not being ironical. We are merely suggesting that the 'message' of this season sounds as a piece of mockery to a world at war – with fierce hatred in the hearts of men. But, the obvious contrast noted, we can look forward and hope – hope that there may be peace on earth before next December. As to goodwill – it will take longer than that to restore the gentle emotion towards an enemy who has exalted torture, massacre, and malevolence as racial ideals and prescribed them with almost incredible violence.

The genius of hate, the perverted Hitler, still presides as fiend incarnate, over a people that shows no signs of renouncing their idolatry. Hitler is still the Father Devilmass. He brings strange gifts to his loutish worshippers. He brings them unceasing bloodshed, privation, hardship, intolerable strain – and promises: such as the promise of Stalingrad before Christmas. Yet Germans fight on. The Russians also. And we; but we fight with renewed hope: based on evidence of things seen; they, with waning hope, turning to acute anxiety. We look forward with confidence, because looking back, we can see how the situation has changed in our favour. Since the dark third Christmas of last year. In this fourth Christmas, the enemy's proud offensive has turned into the defensive.[14]

Notes

1   The Declaration also formed the basis of the United Nations Organisation, which was established after hostilities ceased.

2   Clark-Kennedy, A.E., *London Pride: the Story of a Voluntary Hospital* (1979), pp. 225–26.

3   *Daily Mirror*, 22 May 1942.

4   Julian, F.B., Address to the British Nursing Association, 27 May 1942.

5   Marchant, H., 'Nursing deputation to Whitehall', 9 September 1942.

6   Deputation to House of Commons by fifty-two women's associations, 9 September 1942, reported in *Daily Mirror*, 10 September 1942.

7   *The Lamp Still Burns*, 1943, National Film Archive London.

8   *Ibid.*

9   *Daily Mirror*, 18 August 1942.

10 *Daily Mirror*, 15 May 1941.

11 *The Royal London Hospital Nurses League Review*, no. xi, December 1942.

12 National Archive WO/222/189, letter written by Nurse Johnston.

13 Lowe, R., *The Welfare State in Britain Since 1945* (1993), p. 126.

14 *Daily Mirror*, 24 December 1942.

CHAOS AND CONTROVERSY

A spirit of optimism accompanied New Year celebrations, but although bombing raids on the city were less frequent, they were no less devastating. On 20 January 1943, Sandhurst Road School in Catford was bombed during the school lunch hour, killing thirty-eight children and six members of staff. A further sixty people were injured. London hospitals once again were at the forefront of delivering urgent attention to the wounded. During the same month, Churchill and Roosevelt met in Casablanca to discuss war strategies. Stalin did not attend because he was preoccupied with military campaigns near Stalingrad, where the Russians were demonstrating they were not quite the pushover Hitler had expected. British newspapers were scathing in their reports of Germany's Führer:

> German propaganda on the home front is busy paying compliments mingled with moans to the power of Russian resistance. The Russians are really rough and tough. Russian methods are 'unique.' Russians know how to put up with their own winter and Germans are not used to that severity. Moreover this new Russia is equipped with every modern mechanism. In short, the naughty animal when

attacked, has known how to defend itself. A belated discovery which suggests a criticism of the omniscient Fuehrer. For since Hitler knows everything ought he not to have known all that the German Press and Radio are now proclaiming in a series of war time lectures about the habits of foreign natives? Evidently Hitler hadn't read his guide book and his history.[1]

On 23 January, the British 8th Army entered Tripoli, and on 3 February, Germany's forces surrendered at Stalingrad. German forces were well and truly on the defensive. Meanwhile, Allied forces injured on the battlefields of North Africa were being treated with a new miracle drug, as the widespread clinical testing of penicillin heralded a new era in the history of medicine. The introduction of penicillin completely revolutionised medical treatment and although supplies were limited until later on in the war, the impact of the drug was phenomenal. Initially, the penicillin was used to treat soldiers suffering from venereal disease, but it was also poured liberally onto open wounds, sometimes with a mixture of sulphonamides. Thousands of soldiers' lives were saved by the drug, which had an instant and dramatic effect on all infections. No more deaths from gas-gangrene or suppurating wounds. Every man was back to being fighting fit within a matter of days. Such was the impact of penicillin, Germans were desperate to get hold of the drug by any means. Therefore, as soon as any Allied soldiers were captured by the enemy, the first thing they forced them to do was urinate in a bottle, in the hope that they could extract penicillin from their urine. The drug also had significant consequences for nursing practice. Gone were the days of making hot poultices and giving sponge baths to draw out infection – as Monica Baly recalled:

Good old fashioned nursing care was rendered superfluous. No longer was the doctor saying, 'I can't do anything but nursing will do a great deal.' We had got to the stage when it appeared as if nursing was not doing very much. The patients got better whether they were nursed or not.[2]

With the use of penicillin, military medical teams expected their patients to make a full recovery from most battle injuries and infections. Nurses in the armed forces quickly became used to injecting the foul-smelling ochre-coloured drug into their patients every four hours, and to watching men, who had been expected to die, make a miracle recovery. Even Churchill was successfully treated with penicillin when he contracted pneumonia on a visit to the 8th Army.

Penicillin was not available to British civilian hospitals, however, until after the war.[3] Indeed, across the nation, hospitals were still in crisis, with one northern hospital of 3,000 beds threatening to close because of staff shortages. Most hospital matrons had seemingly learnt nothing in terms of relaxing their disciplinary regimes. The following scenario, reported in the press, illustrated the draconian ethos which pervaded nursing establishments:

A nurse went to a dance in a pair of silver slippers. They had two inch heels. One of the senior nurses saw her. She was penalised because the matron had a rule that no nurse was to wear high heeled shoes. She protested that she had worn them in her free time.

That is typical of the inane, fatuous regulations which some crotchety old matron has the power to impose on her staff. It is also an example of the kind of restriction and vindictive treatment which makes the present young woman regard a hospital as a cross between a nunnery and a gaol.

There have been eternal commissions, committees and reports on the nursing service, and though everyone brings forward evidence of petty, mean restrictions, they still continue.[4]

Other rules included: no flowers allowed in bedrooms, no shoes on floors, nothing allowed on window sills or dressing tables, no baths after 10 p.m. One ex-probationer nurse wrote to the Ministry of Health, complaining:

Life on the wards was one long nightmare. I did my best with work that was entirely new to me, only to be severely reprimanded if anything was wrong, and usually in front of the patients. Sister never tried to help us, she was just there to find fault. Priority was given to the tidying of lockers and straightening beds before the care of patients.[5]

Yet the majority of nurses were prepared to subject themselves to strict discipline whilst they were at work. It was the intrusion into their private lives which irked the most, and the press were clearly on their side:

The outdoor dress must be quiet and unostentatious.

It is time to speak plainly about the treatment of nurses. It is not merely that we need 10,000 nurses at once, and that few will volunteer while conditions are as they are. The matter is much graver than that. We none of us have the right to tolerate for a day longer the petty tyrannies that female sadists, Blimpish specialists and a time-dishonoured tradition inflict on these noble women. It is a reflection on the personal character of those responsible that nurses should be deprived of their liberty as effectively as though they were criminal, punished almost at will, put to unnecessary menial tasks, grossly underpaid, cut off from any healthy private life and continually bullied. The pay is a matter where government action has to be taken – but what of the conditions? Must the government be expected to issue a memorandum before one human being shows consideration and respect for another? If hospital authorities wish for guidance as to how one human being should treat another there is after all, a useful document called a Bible, on sale at all booksellers and very moderately priced.[6]

Not all matrons were draconian, however, and there were plenty who supported their nursing staff with kindness and genuine concern. Within the pages of their diaries and letters, Rose and her friends rarely mentioned ward sisters or their respective matrons. According to their notes, it was the home sister who seemed to rule the roost in their off-duty hours. The home sister checked that rules were being obeyed, decided when toasting time should come to an end, and called for lights out each evening. Their matrons were usually mentioned with a sense of admiration, respect and gratitude. Matron Gladys Hillyers, for example, was much admired by her nurses, especially those who remained in sector hospitals for a considerable time. They were grateful that she made considerable efforts to visit them, and even commissioned a special badge to be given to her sector hospital nurses. Miss Clare Alexander at The London was also renowned for being progressive in character. Old-fashioned disciplinarian matrons were more likely to be found in towns and rural areas, and since British society was changing rapidly, these disciplinarians were continually out of step with the expectations of young women. There were more opportunities because the marriage bar had been lifted, and an influx of American GIs the previous year had lifted the mood of the nation's women. Although resented by some, because their wages were about five times more than the average British soldier, GIs were friendly and generous. They seemed to have a never-ending supply of chewing gum, candy and silk stockings, and were more than happy to spend their ample wages on local women. American base camps held parties, dances and other social events. Glenn Miller's music could be heard across the land, and the British were introduced to the jitterbug. Naturally, young nurses wanted to join in the fun. Yet, confined to their nurses' home with very little free time, they were prevented from doing so. Some enterprising probationers managed to escape their rooms by climbing down drainpipes, clambering across rooftops with the deftness of a cat burglar, or by other means, but they ran the risk of being instantly dismissed if they were caught in the act – despite the fact that hundreds of hospital beds lay empty because of nursing shortages. A situation which was compounded by the fact that measles and scarlet fever epidemics were sweeping the country. It was reported:

There are 2,724 more beds occupied in London County Council's infectious diseases hospitals than last year, and 900 extra nurses are needed, 500 beds are empty. Unless more help is obtained for hospitals, mothers on war work may have to stay at home to nurse their children.

People with an interest in children would be welcome for full or part time work.

Dr Somerville Hastings, Chairman of the Hospitals and Medical Services Committee said yesterday that the work was 'jolly' and there was little risk of infection. Measles presents the greatest problem. Cases are increasing at the rate of a 100 a week and will continue to do so. Scarlet fever has reached its peak but 150 cases a week are being notified compared with 30 a week a year ago. Whooping cough cases are occurring at the rate of 100 a week. There is less fever than before the war, but more than last year and deaths have decreased because of improved treatment.[7]

Grace, who had initially wanted to work at Great Ormond Street, was momentarily tempted to leave St Thomas'. She had recently been enthralled by a story told to her by a children's nurse at the Westminster, of a 5-week-old baby boy who was strapped to a custom-made wooden cross whilst undergoing an operation:

With this cross for his cradle and bandages for his swaddling clothes baby Peter is offered to the steady skilled hands of a senior surgeon at Westminster hospital. Gently but firmly his tiny feet and hands were strapped to the padded cross so that he could not curl his legs or arms as babies do. The operation was for an internal obstruction and it took fifteen minutes. All through it he was soothed by a dummy and the soft caressing hands of the sister who watched over his head. He did not whimper, for a local anaesthetic stopped the pain. Instead he dozed quietly under the strong arc lights. So in the midst of so much death and destruction one young life was saved.[8]

Rose, meanwhile, disappointed by the lack of energy gained from Dr Williams' pink pills, had embarked on an exercise regime. A supposed fitness expert, Dorothy Cooke, had written an article entitled 'Lose that Floppy Feeling'. Rose was not at all sure that she felt floppy, but decided to take Dorothy's advice regardless. The advice was as follows:

First open the window wide. An air bath tones the skin.

Sponge the whole body quickly with a cloth wrung out of cold water.

Rub yourself briskly with a rough towel – rubbing arms and legs upwards towards the heart. Next put on vest and pants and do this exercise.

Stand straight with feet together. Swing left arm up over head and stand on tip toes, stretching as high as possible then lower heels and swing arm down (2): repeat with right arm (3–4); swing both arms up and stretch on tip toes (5) in this position stretch up, counting (6–8); swing arms sideways down and bend knees outward (9); stretch knees again jumping feet apart (10); jump feet together with a little double skip. Repeat four times.[9]

Having hit her hand on the wardrobe twice and jumped on a loose floorboard, Rose was not enamoured with the exercise routine, which was supposed to take a mere five minutes and had taken over ten. She also strongly suspected there may be a rule against jumping on floorboards in the nurses' home. According to her diary, Rose maintained this keep-fit regime for over a month and eventually recorded an improvement in her well-being. By this stage, Rose and her friends had left their probationary years behind them and were all registered nurses. As such, they eagerly anticipated the results of the Rushcliffe Committee and were pleasantly surprised when, in the summer of 1943, the Committee recommended that improved, compulsory national pay scales should be introduced for nurses, with an increased salary divergence between trained and untrained staff. The implementation of these proposals required an additional expenditure of £2.75 million, and half of this cost was borne by the Exchequer. Working hours for nurses were to be limited to ninety-six a fortnight, and in an attempt to improve the distribution of nurses, the Control of Engagement Order, which had applied to other women between the ages of 18–40, was extended to include nurses.

The ramifications of Rushcliffe's proposals, however, were not all positive. Before the introduction of compulsory pay scales, house governors in charge of mental hospitals and sanatoriums had been able to offer nurses higher salaries as an incentive to work in these unfavourable nursing fields. Without this financial inducement, nurses naturally gravitated to general nursing, which increased nursing deficiencies in unpopular and isolated areas, although a clause in the Control of Engagement Order that relinquished nurses from control if they began further post-registration training did improve the midwifery sector. Since most newly qualified nurses did not wish to be controlled by the Ministry of Labour, they chose to train as midwives. Initially, Rushcliffe pay scales did improve nurse recruitment, but these salary improvements were largely negated by the fact that the cost of living had risen by 40 per cent between 1940 and 1943. Moreover, the General Nursing Council (GNC), in league with Ministry of Health officials, decided that the period of nurse training should be extended from three years to four, arguing that a longer training period would improve registered nurse status and thus improve recruitment. Yet it was obvious to all that this decision was economically driven. Rushcliffe had increased pay differentials between trained and untrained nurses. Consequently, it benefitted individual hospitals and the Ministry of Health to keep nurse recruits in training for as long as possible. Senior nurses within the GNC and the Royal College of Nursing also sanctioned the government's 1943 Nurses Act, which prompted outrage in the nursing profession. This controversial Act legitimised assistant nurses, and allowed Christian Science nurses, who had no formal training whatsoever, to adopt the title 'nurse'.

A young nurse named Iris Bower recalled: 'You would have thought the world had caved in the way everyone went on.'[10]

Rose noted with indignation in her diary:

Everyone is very fed up. How could the government betray us in this way? First saying that nurse probationers should train for four years, and then informing us that we might as well not bother because any Tom, Dick or Harry can call themselves nurses without even opening an anatomy book! It makes me want to spit with fury. Why would any girl in their right mind enter the profession?

The indomitable Ethel Bedford-Fenwick, a leading protagonist of the earlier nurse registration movement and editor of the *British Nursing Journal*, was also up in arms:

> It is almost incredible that, after the profession of nursing has existed in England for a quarter of a century, totally ignorant Ministers of the Crown should be permitted to smash up not only the status of an honourable profession but deprive the public of necessary safeguards to health and life.[11]

Whilst registered nurses were understandably outraged at having their status undermined, patient safety was at the heart of their concerns. In fact, the risk of being nursed by an unqualified member of the public who claimed to be a nurse was actually quite high. In 1943 alone, there were at least 115 prosecutions of people who had falsely represented themselves as nurses.

However, despite the professional disappointment caused by the Nurses Act, and the limitations of Rushcliffe's recommendations, there was no doubt that Rushcliffe pay scales did improve nurse recruitment levels. By the time Rushcliffe delivered his second report on 2 December, there was a visible upturn in recruitment figures:

> More than 17,000 nurses in England and Wales are to share pay increases exceeding £500,000 a year. This results from the second report of the Rushcliffe Committee issued yesterday. The Committee have already proposed salary increases totalling £1,500,000 and £2,000,000 a year for female hospital nurses and over £250,000 for midwives, and their present proposals which the Minister of Health has approved will operate from April last.
>
> Six thousand five hundred women, including 1,643 trainees without previous experience were placed in nursing and midwifery vacancies in the five months ended October. And the Ministry of Labour expect that the number of recruits will soon pass the 10,000 mark. Giving these figures in a speech at Leeds yesterday, Mr Malcolm

McCorquodale Parliamentary Secretary to the Ministry said the number of vacancies filled in October alone was over 2,000.

'We are well on the way to filling a very considerable number of the vacancies in the general nursing field' he said. 'But we haven't broken the back of the problem so far as it affects the special services such as tuberculosis sanatoria, mental hospitals, fever hospitals and midwifery.'[12]

Advertisements in the popular press extolled new nursing conditions and were considerably more appealing to young girls. They included training with pay, holidays with pay, free uniforms, new salary scales, pension schemes and a wide range of specialist subjects. If the omnipresent matter of unbelievably strict discipline and extreme subservience was overlooked, the work could almost be deemed attractive. But as Monica Baly asserted:

> There is no doubt about it, the discipline exerted in the schools of nursing was too strict. At St Thomas' for example, they were being told to polish their brasses to the glory of God in 1938. But in 1941 they were no way going to polish their brasses to the glory of God.[13]

Certainly, by 1943, nurse recruits were not keen to do any polishing, brasses or otherwise. There were a variety of careers open to young girls and women had undoubtedly gained new freedoms and a sense of independence. Nursing was institutional, and within the hospitals, life and routines had ossified. Therefore, although Rushcliffe pay scales had prompted more girls to take up nursing, retention was still a huge problem. Furthermore, as Monica Dickens claimed, the average nurse had little idea of what was happening in the outside world. Diaries of nurses barely mentioned politics or the state of war. Family members, sweethearts, patients and doctors, medical and nursing treatments all appeared sporadically within their literary outputs, but not one included the fact that the Russians were embroiled in the Battle of Kursk in July, or that Italy surrendered to the Allies on 8 September 1943. Ironically, given her preoccupation with glamour, romance and fitness,

Rose knew more about international affairs than her friends. Thanks to her other hobby, which involved emulating film stars and attending cinemas, she gleaned a substantial amount of information from Pathé newsreels, which were routinely shown at every cinema across the country. Clearly some newsreel content was primarily propaganda, but Rose was convinced that most of it could be believed. Moreover, if she could remember any details of news reports she would often relay them to her friends.

As yet another wartime Christmas approached, however, it was the problem of providing adequate gifts that dominated nurses' diaries. Flo noted in her diary that it was becoming difficult to find good quality toys for children:

> The government has banned the sale of toys containing more than ten per cent metal to save metal for war production, and there is not a park railing to be seen in the whole of London. I will have to knit some soft cuddly toys for my nephews and a bed jacket for my mother. I saw a bargain in a shop window on the high street yesterday – one coupon for 4ozs of Arifona art silk knitting crepe 7.1/2d per oz. It's usually sold at 10d an oz. I don't suppose they have many colours but I don't think mother will mind much. As for the children, they always seem happy with whatever they get.

Rose, meanwhile, was busy writing a Christmas letter to Harold on a special lightweight air-graph designed by Aircraftsman Sherbourne. As usual, her head was full of romance, and she provided her fiancé with a comprehensive list of the films she'd seen in the past few months, courtesy of the Odeon's free ticket supply for nurses. Listed as her favourite was *The Gentle Sex*, a semi-documentary film which followed the fortunes of women and war. Rose also wrote of a romantic but true story, which had captured her attention earlier in the year:

> In Moscow, one post office employee Lydia Gardieva sent a letter with her blood bottle:

Dear soldier – I do not know you, but if my blood gives you life and strength to fight the enemy I'll be happy.

She received an answer from Lieutenant Colonel Vinogradoff who had the transfusion. Other letters followed, then a long silence. Lydia supposed him killed till one day she wept with joy at receiving a long awaited letter, which told of an extraordinary coincidence. The Colonel was severely wounded and was again given a transfusion. And again he found that the donor was Lydia. Doctors, nurses and patients were so amazed that they called a meeting at which, said the Colonel in a letter to Lydia 'Your name, my sister, whose blood flows in my veins, was spoken with that love which one can only know when one is at the front.'[14]

Over at St Thomas', Grace was planning a cookery evening to make gifts of food for her relatives. In the nurses' home of The London, Gladys was reading a particularly forceful and dramatic newspaper article penned by someone called Lord Simon, entitled: 'We must populate or perish!' Lord Simon was apparently a leading eugenics expert, who firmly believed the whole of Britain to be doomed unless every Briton of child-bearing age went forth promptly and multiplied at a rapid rate.[15] Gladys crumpled the newspaper and threw it in the bin. She had not yet managed to read all the books on her list, but she had read enough to know that eugenics ideology was inextricably linked with Hitler and his theories of racial purity and supremacy. Besides, as far as she could tell, there had already been something of a population explosion since the arrival of the American GIs.

Teased by some Brits for being 'over-sexed, overpaid and over here', GIs were undoubtedly extremely good-natured, and their immense generosity made Christmas 1943 a special event for many British families. In addition to holding highly popular Christmas parties for British children, GIs also bestowed a variety of luxury gifts on ordinary families. This Christmas was also a time when the Allies could, at long last, look forward to the liberation of Europe and victory in the Pacific. Thus, President Roosevelt chose Christmas Eve 1943 to announce that the Allies would be fighting on a second front the following year, under the command of General Eisenhower. He also had a special message for Americans fighting far from home:

> Tonight on Christmas Eve, all men and women who love Christmas are thinking of that ancient town and the star of faith that shone there more than nineteen centuries ago. American boys are fighting today in snow covered mountains, in malarial jungles, and on blazing deserts, they are fighting for the thing for which they struggle. I think it is best symbolized by the message that came out of Bethlehem.[16]

Notes

1 *Daily Mirror*, 9 January 1943.
2 Dr Monica Baly, *Frontline Females*, vol. 2.
3 For a comprehensive analysis of the penicillin story, please see: Neushul, P., 'Fighting research', in Cooter, R., Harrison, M., & Sturdy, S., *Medicine War and Modernity* (1998), pp. 203–19.
4 *Daily Mirror*, 1 March 1943.
5 Extract of letter written to Ministry of Health and later published in Cohen, J., *The Minority Report on the Recruitment of Nurses* (1948), pp. 64–74.
6 *Daily Mirror*, 1 March 1943.
7 *Daily Mirror*, 17 February 1943.
8 *Daily Mirror*, 27 January 1943.
9 Cooke, D., 'Lose that floppy feeling', 21 September 1943.
10 Bower, I., Recollections published in Royal College of Nursing, *History of Nursing Journal*, vol. 3, no. 3 (1990), pp. 52–56.
11 *British Journal of Nursing*, May 1945.
12 *Daily Mirror*, 3 December 1943.
13 Baly, M., Oral history interview with author, May 1995.
14 *Daily Mirror*, 6 March 1943.
15 *Ibid.*, 7 December 1943.
16 President Franklin D. Roosevelt, National Broadcast to the Nation, 24 December 1943.

13

THE MINI BLITZ

In early 1944, preparations for a second front prompted a myriad of training exercises for Allied troops stationed across Britain, and the implementation of detailed medical support strategies within military nursing services. These plans were hampered, however, by new government regulations. The previous year, in an attempt to alleviate civilian nursing shortages – and as a result of lengthy discussions between the Ministry of Labour and the War Office – the Ministry of Health had placed considerable restrictions on nurse conscription. Henceforth, matrons, assistant matrons, sister tutors, practising midwives, district nurses, sanatorium nurses, sick children's nurses and mental health nurses were all prevented from joining the armed forces. In cases of severe nursing shortages, civilian hospitals were also allowed to request postponement of 'call up' with regard to nurses not in the aforementioned categories.[1] Naturally, the War Office was reluctant to agree to these restrictions, since it meant that only newly qualified nurses could now enter the forces. With the need to provide adequate medical support on a second front, these restrictions were also extremely ill-timed. Military medical units needed experienced nurses who could cope under pressure, supervise medical orderlies and take the initiative in difficult situations. Therefore, to be depleted in number and deprived of experienced nurses at such a crucial time placed enormous pressure on military medical staff.

On the Home Front, Ministry of Health officials had embarked on public health education programmes in an attempt to prevent the spread of influenza and tuberculosis, and curb the rising number of venereal disease cases. Most of the lectures regarding the latter problem were aimed at young boys. Mr T.H. Clark, for instance, a physical training master at Enfield Technical College, spoke frankly to large numbers of boys using large diagrams from anatomy books and a series of films produced by the Central Council of Health Education:

> There is no reason for you boys to talk a lot of silly nonsense about the reproductive organs of the body. You can refer to them as you refer to your eyes or ears, and you can speak about them to your doctor, your parson and your mother and father. There is nothing alarming about female organs. There are many marvels of the human machine, and if you spoil them you can't grow others. If you damage your bodies you may do harm to others, for many generations. We are talking straight. You have to look after yourselves. Self-interference is morally wrong. It brings ugly thoughts, in which evil effects lie. Victims do not develop full personality or character, and the bad habit may stand after marriage. Now about relationships with girls. Syphilis can be handed down, because the infection is caused by a specific germ. Experimenters in sex may be infected with venereal disease. Some of you boys may leave your homes for other towns or to enter the services. There are a lot of girls about today who are grateful to Servicemen, but you must not expect this gratitude to be expressed in bad sex. If a girl is easy for you, more likely she has been easy for others, in which case she may be a source of infection to you.[2]

Sex education was a new innovation, however, and many adults believed that such talks would encourage the young to have sex rather than deter them from promiscuity. Lectures about sexual relationships also showed in graphic detail the development of babies before birth, in order to highlight the consequences of unprotected sex. National newspapers frequently reported extracts from such lectures, but were required to tread a very fine line between providing valuable information on the one hand, and prompting moral outrage on the other.

Rose and her friends held different opinions on the matter, as she recorded in her diary:

> Grace says the more people talk about sex the more they want to find out for themselves what it's like. Flo agrees with her and says more youngsters will be encouraged to have sex down back alleys. Gladys is unsure – and at any rate most men down her way pay prostitutes for sex. Her mother says prostitutes go out looking like 'Tom Tits on a pump handle' whatever that means. Personally I think they should give more talks about sex to young girls – even if they don't get V.D. they are still the ones left holding the baby! I've told Harold we are not having sex until our wedding night so that's that. A girl needs to know she has security before getting in the family way.

An emphasis on public health dominated the first few months of 1944, in part to curb epidemics, but also to provide a fit cohort of new recruits for the armed forces. Newspapers were full of numerous stories of strong Allied advances, and on 6 June, British and American forces landed on the beaches of Normandy. Seven days later, on 13 June, Germans attacked London and southern England with pilot-less flying bombs, heralding a period which became known as the mini Blitz. These flying bombs were frequently launched in broad daylight and could not be detected by radar. Carrying a 1-ton warhead, the V-1 travelled at 350mph to a preset target. Nicknamed Doodlebugs, a total of 9,521 V-1 flying bombs were fired on London and the south. Anti-aircraft fire and Royal Air Force fighters destroyed 4,621 of these. The later V-2 rockets were much faster and more difficult to destroy, because they could travel at supersonic speed; around 5,000 of these rockets were aimed specifically at London. The V-1s and V-2s were seen as more sinister than the previous heavy bombing raids, since there was no warning of their arrival. It was virtually impossible, therefore, for anyone to take cover before they exploded. As Dr Arthur Walker of St Thomas' Hospital recalled: 'It was a very anxious time because you heard them coming, then they went quiet, then they exploded. One day a block of flats was hit just north of Hammersmith – there were appalling injuries.'[3]

A nurse on duty that day described one of the victims:

> We had casualties in. We had one dear old lady come in, I remember from Peabody buildings in Hammersmith. She was very very dirty, a sweet old soul but she was dirty and smelt dreadful. She had a terrific gash on her leg. I had to get her clothes off and she apologised in a broad cockney accent, 'I'm sorry luv, I haven't had my bath this week, but I have washed up as far as possible and I've washed down as far as possible.' I remember the casualty doctor saying, 'I wish she had washed [her] possible sometimes because she did smell absolutely dreadful.'[4]

A nursing sister named Miss Musared at The London also described an injured woman in her care, a victim injured by a flying bomb which had landed on Bethnal Green:

> While I was 'Sister Gloucester' I had the first flying bomb casualty, a woman with multiple wounds and a severely mutilated arm. It took us forty eight hours to get out of severe shock. Her chief concern then was for her family. The almoner was able to trace her husband to a rest centre and found that one boy had been killed trying to save his sister, and her other two children were severely injured. An interlude of two days followed. Then these flying bombs started coming in at the rate of a hundred a day.[5]

St Thomas' was hit several times by Doodlebugs during July, but for the most part damage was not severe, as reported in the national press:

London buildings damaged in recent flying bomb attacks include St Thomas' Hospital, Palmerston House in Old Broad Street; and Spurgeon's Baptist Training College, in South Norwood. The bomb on St Thomas' fortunately fell on an empty wing which had been damaged in earlier raids on London. It brought down a great deal of masonry. Deep beneath this block is the Nuffield ward, which had been reinforced against blast. None of the patients in the ward was injured or even shaken. Neighbouring residents were cut by glass.[6]

The London Hospital was not so fortunate. On 3 August, Miss Alexander, Matron at The London, was working in her office in the early hours when a V-1 flying bomb landed on the hospital. Medical student Oldershaw was fire-watching on the roof:

We knew it was coming. Many had gone over. One had just landed nearby and, simultaneously with its explosion, we heard the engine of another almost on top of us and the 'imminent danger' warning of the Klaxons. Then I saw it! It fell out of low clouds and I watched it diving for the hospital, heard the final roar and the sound of walls falling, shouting in the streets, doors opening and banging, all merged into seeing the building blazing with light through a cloud of rising dust. Sister Gloucester, who had been lying awake in a room on the ground floor, dived under her bedclothes. Plaster, broken glass and the cupboard doors showered on my bed, all lights went out and my door jammed. The house governor, who was in his flat on the ground floor of Alexandra Home and also still awake, had heard the bomb coming, the engine stop, and then the swish of it descending. A crash followed. The ceiling came down and his wardrobe fell on top of him. The lights went off. He couldn't find his torch and so spent the next few desperate moments hunting for his trousers and his little Yorkshire terrier, which had been sleeping on his bed in total darkness.[7]

A nurse on duty at The London that night compiled the following report for Matron:

At 1.35am I was sitting at the table in the middle of the ward. Everything was quiet; all the patients were asleep. Suddenly I heard the sound of a flying bomb. The engine stopped and then I heard it whistling through the air and realised that it could hardly avoid hitting us. A moment later there was a terrific explosion, complete darkness, the crash of falling masonry and the rush of water. Complete silence followed, and for a moment I feared that all my patients had been killed. So I began to grope my way in the darkness towards the lobby to fetch my hurricane lamp, but a soldier struck a match and I saw my torch lying on the table, switched it on, and he exclaimed, 'Oh nurse, you had better sit down.' (I was bleeding from various cuts and scratches on my face and arm). I went to the patients near me and asked if they were alright. All answered cheerfully. Then, leaving the torch, I took the matches and went to the lobby for the hurricane lamp where I met Miss Burgess. I told her that I had lost my spectacles. She came back with me, and we went to the far end of the ward to see if the rest of the patients were alright. There we discovered a huge crater, and realised that the bed containing a soldier, had completely disappeared.[8]

Dr Clark-Kennedy reported that:

I made my way across the quadrangle, which was piled high with broken masonry and rubble. I found the patients in Gloucester ward quiet and calm. In the lobby, water was cascading down from the roof and a fireman asked me for a dose of Broad-bents in case he caught a cold![9]

The bomb had crashed into the fourth-floor kitchen before moving downwards between the wards. Kitchen equipment had descended through lobbies into the basement, creating huge holes in the ground. One of the main water tanks was hanging over a large crater. Two nurses were discovered injured in the gardens and were quickly brought in to safety. Bombs were falling rapidly, so children and other patients were transported to the basement. ARP workers, along with medical staff and hospital surveyors, struggled against descending floodwater to restore some semblance of safety and order. Later that night, Stepney power station was hit and the hospital was in total darkness until emergency generators restored lights. Two patients were killed by falling masonry and buried under the rubble, but miraculously no one else was hurt. The bomb had severely damaged a nurses' home, covered walkways and a temporary radiology building. Blackout curtains had been destroyed and nearly every window shattered or blown in. Large doors had been wrenched off their hinges and debris scattered across hospital grounds. After this harrowing night, the doctors' kitchen surprised everyone by producing a luxury breakfast of bacon and eggs for patients and medical staff. Even more surprisingly, the House Governor's report concluded:

While the damage to the hospital has been heavy, and there has been a great loss of equipment and stores, the governors will be pleased to know that the hospital never closed for the admission of patients, and by the evening there were two hundred and sixty three beds ready. There was no confusion of any kind, and I would like to pay a tribute to all staff, medical and nursing, lay and domestic, who worked calmly and most efficiently through the early hours of 3rd August and the trying days since.[10]

Gladys wrote in her notebook:

Some of us were superficially wounded by shards of glass, but most escaped injury. One of the char ladies hurt her arm, but nothing serious. I must admit I find these doodle bugs menacing and fearsome. It's that period of silence before the thunderous roar that gets my heart racing and I feel as though I might vomit with the sheer terror of it all. The patients are remarkably calm and I know I must appear so, for if they realise I am scared stiff, all panic might ensue.

Rose was more forthright in her notes: 'Blasted Germans! As if we haven't been bombed enough. I hope someone makes them pay for all the damage they've caused.'

Despite inflicting severe damage on hospitals and other buildings, casualty rates from V-1 flying bombs were relatively low. However, when the first V-2 rockets landed on London on 8 September, casualty rates rose dramatically. Yet again, London's East End was the prime target area. Press reports deliberately downplayed the impact of the V-2s, and wrongly stated the distance they were able to travel in an attempt to fool the Germans. Furthermore, many of the V-2 rockets experienced mechanical problems, and due to the speed of impact, damage was often inflicted deep underground.

On 10 November, a V-2 rocket landed in a crowded market place in Petticoat Lane. Dr Clark-Kennedy was on duty at The London:

Over two hundred casualties were brought into the hospital that night, it was full to overflowing. Extra beds were put up in every ward. A few days later another fell on Aldgate. Again the receiving room was filled with stretcher cases and walking wounded, and four of the wards standing empty had to be opened. Students carried up mattresses and casualties were parked on the floor, irrespective of age and sex, waiting their surgical turn.[11]

Rocket attacks continued to increase in frequency. However, the Royal Air Force were able to destroy some V-2s before they reached Britain or other targets:

Specially picked and briefed Spitfire pilots yesterday planted all their bombs in a Dutch railway station and siding used to park V-2 supply trains. Typhoon bombers, based in Belgium bombed railway wagons in marshalling yards believed to be laden with V-2s on their way to The Hague.[12]

In addition to coping with rocket attack victims from June 1944 onwards, British hospitals were also dealing with casualties evacuated from the second front. Most of the wounded were evacuated by ship, but at least 400 a day were airlifted back to England. However, some of the casualties arriving home by sea arrived in critical condition. Sergeant James Anderson wrote to Normandy to protest:

My Dear Brigadier,

I am writing to confirm our conversation about the serious condition of several patients who arrived at Alverstoke Emergency Hospital Scheme hospitals in convoys last Friday morning and append to several specific cases. I feel that the medical officers who are evacuating cases from hospitals on the other side do not realise that the patients may be on board landing craft for two or even three days before they reach a hospital on this side, and during these two or three days the patient's condition may deteriorate considerably. For example two cases had gas gangrene by the time we got them. Again Plaster of Paris covers a multitude of sins and when this is applied the notes should describe the severity of the patient's injuries accurately. When a case comes to hospital near a beach, if it is in POP that doctor may easily look at this plaster – see that it is alright – ask if it is comfortable and then pass it on. Two of the patients should really have been held by the hospital on the beach. Almost without exception the medical attention that the patients have had has been beyond reproach but I note one exception below.

This patient had a terrible wound of the left buttock and thigh. Two thirds of the circumference of the limb including the femur was just not there. The early operation note stated that debridement of the wound had been carried out, a Tobruk plaster had been applied over a Thomas Splint and then he had been sent on his way. In the first place his leg should have been amputated if not at the FSU certainly in the General Hospital but the 3118 gave the hospital no idea of the severity of the wound.

I don't wish to be highly critical and the forward medical officers and surgeons have really done a splendid job. I merely wish to warn you that in their anxiety to keep beds available for fresh cases there is a danger that cases are being evacuated whilst they are still unfit for the arduous journey that lies ahead of them. I feel that it is possible that the officers who evacuate them may not realise that it takes so long for them to get to hospitals in England.[13]

Reports from Normandy, however, were generally positive. Medical techniques were extremely effective, the wonder drug penicillin was widely administered and there was no shortage of fresh blood. In addition to Allied personnel, military medical teams were also caring for enemy soldiers. Most of these soldiers were young and impressionable, and had succumbed to German propaganda. They all appeared to be under the impression that England was already occupied by Germans. One nurse described this situation when writing to her matron from the front line:

The very first patient on D-Day was a German officer – I can't remember his rank – an army officer with shrapnel in his buttocks, and he demanded to be taken to German occupied England. On being told that no part of England was occupied – it took a lot to convince him of this – he became very frantic with fright because he had been told that English doctors operated on prisoners of war without an anaesthetic. It took five of us to hold him down to give him an anaesthetic. Some of the soldiers were most peculiar, especially the S.S. officers. They didn't want to survive. Some of them pulled out their intravenous tubes when they were having a blood transfusion. They just wanted to die for the Fuhrer and they jolly well did. They used to walk around and blow their tops. They were very arrogant. When we were busy nursing we had bed, stretcher, bed, stretcher, in the reception room; the place had been a little school and we had stretchers galore. You could hardly put your feet between them. We were luckily wearing our battledress kit because the Germans used to mess on the floor, and we had to put our gaiters on so that we didn't get the bottom of our trousers filthy. They were all in a very queer state.[14]

Another nurse recorded that many of the captured Germans were under the age of 19:

They had been wounded a long time. They were very young boys. They were seventeen and eighteen and on their notes they had two years' service, some of them. They had the most ghastly wounds. This was where you could tell that the German medical treatment wasn't good. Amputations – limbs had been just chopped off. Suppurating wounds, necrosed bones (dead bone) and they looked terrible.[15]

Over 265,000 Germans were killed or wounded, and 350,000 were captured as prisoners of war during the bid to free France from German occupation.[16]

Yet, despite the Allied advance, the Germans were reluctant to surrender even though they were under attack from both sides. The Russians in the east were marching towards Germany's heartland, and the American, British and French armies had advanced as far as the frontiers of the Reich. Simultaneously, Allied air raids on Germany were imposing and debilitating. Short of manpower, and with diminishing levels of industrial production, Germany was in the process of being reduced to rubble. In an attempt to regain control of his western flank, Hitler propelled his military machine towards Antwerp, hoping to split American and British forces. Thus, on 16 December, Germany launched a major counteroffensive, which became known as the Battle of the Bulge because of the bulge it created in the American lines. Initially, American forces sustained heavy losses and fell back, but against the odds they held fast and the Germans were unable to break through. Eisenhower instructed Patton to attack the German left flank, and promptly placed American units cut off by communications disruptions under the command of Montgomery.

A coordinated response was maintained and the Battle of the Bulge became the largest land battle fought by Americans during the whole of the Second World War.

Back in Britain, as the year drew to a close, an influenza epidemic gripped the Home Front. A Ministry of Health circular gave advice to the general public, as follows:

> Every available service in Britain – including youth organisations and civil defence workers is to be mobilised to fight the country's latest enemy, influenza. Worry and missing meals are the two main things which seriously damage people's ability to keep free from infection and to fight influenza when they fall victim. So the spearhead of the all-out attack on the epidemic is to be the home of an influenza district where the housewife is overburdened; and the homes of people taken ill who have no one to give them proper care. Arrangements are to be announced locally. Youth organisations are to organise teams of boys and girls to do the shopping for influenza sufferers and look after very young children. British restaurants will have hot meals ready for collection by fit members of the family. Rest centres and first aid posts staffs, school nurses and health visitors will be on duty to help smooth out difficulties in homes where there is illness.[17]

Rose and twenty other nurses at The London were amongst the thousands who caught influenza and were laid up in the nurses' sick bay. Gladys, who had suffered during the previous year's epidemic, remained steadfastly immune to the latest strain of the virus. Rose, who had nursed several patients with post-influenza pneumonia, woke up on 22 December with a raging temperature, sore throat and thumping headache. The following day she was admitted to the nurses' sick bay, where she stayed throughout the Christmas festivities. Amongst other gifts, Gladys brought her friend details of the day's radio broadcasts:

BBC Radio programme schedule for 23rd December 1944:

9am Welcome Yule – music for Christmas tide.

9.30 music

10.15 Service

10.30 Music while you work

11am Saturday morning prom

12.30 music

1.15 Backs to the Land

1.30 Band music

2pm Organ Serenade

2.30 music

3.30 musical shows of 1944

4pm Spelling Bee

4.30 Music while you work

5pm Welsh

5.20 Children's hour

6.30 The World Goes By

6.55 Those were the days

7.45 A Week in Westminster

8pm Music Hall with Tommy Fields, Charlie Kunz, Issy Bonn, Anna Neagle and Rob Wilton

9.30 Play – Michael and Mary

10.30 Evening Prayers

10.45 Dance music[18]

Rose was singularly unimpressed, as Gladys woefully acknowledged:

It was quite disturbing to see Rose, normally so full of beans, lying insipid and wan in the hushed sick bay. I thought she might summon enough strength to go to the common room and listen to the radio, but she is languishing in bed with a face as red as a pillar box. I straightened her pillows and dabbed her forehead with a cold compress but like most nurses she is a poor patient and is feeling very sorry for herself. I encouraged her to drink plenty of water and gave her a pile of books, a radio timetable and a copy of this month's nursing journal. She says she can't possibly read because her eyes are stinging so, and her head is throbbing. She told me she just wants to crawl into a corner and die quietly. I told her to stop behaving as though she were Melanie Wilkes from *Gone with the Wind* – and sternly informed her that we need all the nurses we can get so she can't possibly die. This did raise a smile.

Leaving her friend's bedside, Gladys made her way home for a pre-Christmas visit. Gladys' sisters were gathered around the kitchen table talking about the new Butler Education Act. Apparently, there was a lot of talk in the East End about education for all and a future classless society. Gladys dismissed this as total nonsense. But despite Gladys' misgivings, the main thrust of the new Education Act aimed to provide state education for all children, divide primary, secondary and further education into distinct age ranges and implement administrative reform. As President of the Board of Education and subsequent Minister of Education, Mr R.A. Butler had adopted a pragmatic approach to reform. He had carefully sifted through educational reports, analysed relevant debates, examined the needs of industry and public service, visited schools and training colleges, and sought the advice of those who worked with children in juvenile courts and youth groups. He summarised his main view in the House of Commons as follows:

> British education goes winding on, like some track up the mountain side of our civilisation, ever ascending and ever providing the traveller with broader views and widening prospects. But alas, like many mountain paths, it ceases abruptly when the children reach the age of fourteen, just when the views are becoming most interesting.[19]

Given his personal viewpoint, it was not surprising that the 1944 Education Act included plans to raise the school leaving age to 15, and at a later date to 16 years. The fact that the Act was passed at all was a major achievement, since Butler had failed to gain the support of his prime minister and many of the coalition backbenchers. Indeed, opposition to educational reform diluted and in some cases negated many of Butler's original proposals, yet regardless of this erosion the Act did represent a major advance in education policy.[20]

The changes implemented as a result of this reform had significant implications for all children, in all walks of life. The nursing profession in particular benefitted enormously from improved education, and pre-nursing courses were introduced in a number of secondary schools.

But like many others across the country at this time, Gladys dismissed notions of educational meritocracy and a fairer society as pipe dreams. Focussing her attention on getting ready for Christmas, she spent the afternoon making paper chain decorations from old newspapers, just as she had the previous year. Her sisters were teasing each other and competing to list as many film stars and entertainers as they could possibly remember. As she painted and pasted the bits of scrap paper, she fervently prayed that this would be the last wartime Christmas.

Notes

1   Imperial War Museum, K9775, p. 6.
2   Clark, T.H., *Sex Education for Boys*: lecture given to 370 boys at Enfield Technical College, 3 December 1943.
3   Walker, A., Oral history testimony, Imperial War Museum Sound Archive ref: IWM/17977/2/1-2.
4   BBC Radio 4, *Frontline Females*, vol. 1.
5   Clark-Kennedy, A.E., *London Pride* (1979), p. 229.
6   *Liverpool Daily Post*, 25 July 1944.
7   Clark-Kennedy, A.E., *op. cit.*, p. 230.
8   *Ibid.*, pp. 230–31.
9   *Ibid.*, p.232.
10 *Ibid.*, p.233.
11 *Ibid.*
12 *Daily Mirror*, 12 December 1944.
13 National Archive, WO/222/176.
14 *Frontline Females*, vol. 2, quoted in Starns, P., *Nurses at War* (2000), pp. 100–01.

15 *Ibid.*, p. 101.
16 Overy, R., *Why the Allies Won* (1995), p. 176.
17 Ministry of Health Circular, December 1944.
18 BBC Archives.
19 Hansard House of Commons Debates, 5th series, 6 June 1942, col 1431.
20 For a comprehensive assessment of the impact, merits and drawbacks of the 1944 Butler Education Act, please see: Lowe, R., *The Welfare State in Britain Since 1945* (1993), pp. 196–303.

14

VICTORY

During the Battle of the Bulge, a combination of swift and substantial Allied reinforcements and isolated bouts of heroism successfully halted the German advance. Difficult terrain, bad weather and fuel shortages had impeded German progress, and once weather conditions improved in late December the Allies were able to bring fighter planes to bear on the situation. By January 1945, therefore, the Germans were in retreat. Subsequent battles in the Rhineland in February and March inflicted major defeats on Germany, and remaining German units were clearly in disarray and imbued with a sense of defeatism.

In London, however, relentless Doodlebug attacks were still causing carnage. On 3 February, the press reported:

Dust was still settling on the tattered night clothes of a fifteen month old baby when rescue workers found its body partly covered by bricks. The baby was dead and lay a few yards from the debris under which its mother – wife of Driver Clarence Munro, now serving in Italy – lay trapped with her other child. For hours while rescue squads dug to contact them Mrs Grace Munro, the soldiers' mother stood by. Only once did she leave – to send a telegram to her soldier son. 'There's no

hope for them' she sobbed, as the squads continued the search. The
bomb wrecked many houses, blasted a nearby church, a town hall and
a police station. Seven hours afterwards another V-2 bomb had fallen.
Mr Alfred Barwick was still pacing up and down outside the ruins
of his home waiting for news of his wife, who lay buried there. He,
like many other husbands had been called from work when the bomb
exploded. In another incident, four hundred boys at a grammar school
behaved with great calmness when it was damaged by a V-2 bomb.
Only a few were injured.[1]

Flo and Grace were both injured in a rocket attack during their off-duty
hours, whilst leisurely walking along the embankment. Flo sustained a
fractured arm as she fell and Grace was hit on her shoulder by falling
masonry. On 8 March, 110 women and children were killed as they
queued to buy rabbit meat in Smithfield Market. Most fell through the
shattered buildings onto railway lines below.

Rose, fully restored to health after her bout of flu, wrote to her aunt:

Rockets come over in quick succession – there's no time to do
anything to avoid them. They travel so fast nobody can hear them
coming. It is terrifying. One minute everything is fine, the next death
and destruction. Newspapers are full of dreadful stories. Gladys, who
loves reading and likes to know what's going on, has stopped reading
the papers altogether. Our maternity cases have been sent to Hitchin
for safety and the children to the Royal Northern. We also have a
growing problem at the hospital because so many patients have lost
their homes they cannot be discharged. Our almoner is overloaded
with work and I'm quite convinced she is heading for a nervous
break-down.

In the early weeks of March, V-2s fell near the London Hospital annexe
in Brentwood and in Commercial Road. On 27 March, the last V-2
rockets fell on London and the south-east. Hughes Mansions in Vallance
Road, Stepney received a direct hit and over 100 people were killed.

Many more were injured. The majority of these were admitted to The London:

> At 7am a black cloud suddenly rose up just north of the hospital, followed a split second later by a roar. A rocket had fallen on a block of flats in the long suffering Vallance Road. A few minutes later, casualties on stretchers and walking wounded badly cut by flying glass crowded in through the main entrance of the hospital. Before long the mortuary was full, the dead lying outside, while a queue formed up seeking to identify relatives. Matron spoke to some of them and the mask like face of a soldier who had returned from the front that morning to find his entire family destroyed remains imprinted on her memory.[2]

Newspapers hailed the bravery of ARP workers and survivors, but also highlighted the growing problem of homelessness:

> She returns to life, but not to a home. Twenty six year old Mrs Esther Boor lies in a coat of white armour in bed at the London Hospital, a very proud and worried woman. Proud because with her neck broken and enclosed in plaster from the waist up, she gave birth to a fine baby boy of 7lb 9oz. Worried because when she comes out of hospital she may have nowhere to go. Her husband Robert, a £5 a week drayman in a local brewery has told her that the authorities could not find them a house to replace the one in Grosvenor Road, demolished with the family's possessions when the bomb which broke Mrs Boor's neck fell. Mrs Boor has a three year old daughter Jean, who has to share a bed with her father in his parents' home in Elm Park. In the George ward at the London hospital they call Mrs Boor their miracle patient. Her head is tilted back to mend her broken spine, and she can only stare at one little area of the ward ceiling. In two weeks they are going to take that plaster cast off Mrs Boor, perhaps for good.[3]

Many homeless people had taken to pitching makeshift tents in parks and areas of wasteland, others were living in seriously overcrowded conditions with relatives or friends. Consequently, the need to provide adequate housing for those who had been bombed out of their homes became a government priority in the final months of the war. By April, an Allied victory in Europe was assured, and on 30 April, Hitler committed suicide, blaming all and sundry for the German defeat. On 2 May, German forces in Italy surrendered, and by 8 May the German High Command had capitulated. The actual signing of the German surrender took place at 2 a.m. on 7 May, and by midnight on the same day people across Britain were celebrating like never before. Public holidays were granted for 8 and 9 May and street parties were in full swing up and down the country. Church bells rang out loudly and joyously across the land, and Britain's naval vessels sounded a siren of salute in honour of the long-awaited victory.

Rose, Gladys and Flo were amongst the loud, flag-waving, raucous revellers heading for Trafalgar Square, where people were enthusiastically dancing, hugging and kissing each other. Truck drivers beeped their horns as they overloaded their vehicles with delighted men, women and children, many of whom were loudly singing the national anthem. Rose and Gladys jumped excitedly into the fountains and embraced total strangers, before congregating on the Mall and Buckingham Palace to hear King George VI. His moving speech focussed on thanksgiving:

Today we give thanks to Almighty God for a great deliverance. Speaking from our Empire's oldest capital city, war battered but never for one moment daunted or dismayed – speaking from London, I ask you to join with me in that act of thanksgiving … Let us remember those who will not come back: their constancy and courage in battle, their sacrifice and endurance in the face of a merciless enemy; let us remember the men in all the services and the women in all the services, who have laid down their lives. We have come to the end of our tribulation and they are not with us at the moment of our rejoicing. Then let us salute in proud gratitude the great host of the living who have brought us to victory. I cannot praise them to the measure of each one's service, for in a total war, the efforts of all rise to the same noble height, and all are devoted to the common purpose.

Armed or unarmed, men and women, you have fought and striven and endured to your utmost. No-one knows that better than I do, and as your King, I thank with a full heart those who bore arms so valiantly on land and sea, or in the air, and all civilians who, shouldering their many burdens, have carried them unflinchingly without complaint.

With those memories in our minds, let us think what it was that has upheld us through nearly six years of suffering and peril. The knowledge that everything was at stake: our freedom, our independence, our very existence as a people; but the knowledge also that in defending ourselves we were defending the liberties of the whole world; that our cause was the cause not of this nation only, not of the Empire and Commonwealth only, but of every land where freedom is cherished and law and liberty go hand in hand ... There is great comfort in the thought that the years of darkness and danger in which the children of our country have grown up are over and, please God, forever. We shall have failed and the blood of our dearest will have flowed in vain if the victory which they died to win does not lead to a lasting peace, founded on justice and good will.

To that, then, let us turn our thoughts to this day of just triumph and proud sorrow, and then take up our work again, resolved as a people to do nothing unworthy of those who died for us, and to make the world such a world as they would have desired for their children and for ours. This is the task to which now honour binds us. In the hour of danger we humbly committed our cause into the hand of God and he has been our strength and shield. Let us thank him for his mercies and in this hour of victory commit ourselves and our new task to the guidance of that same strong hand.

Celebrations continued non-stop, throughout the nights and days that followed. But just as the king had acknowledged in his speech, victory was also tinged with sadness, as Rose recorded in her diary:

Nobody can truly appreciate the wonderful atmosphere on the streets of London today unless they've lived through the hell of the blitz. No more wearing tin hats, shaking broken glass out of my shoes, tending patients mutilated by bombs, rushing to take cover under tables, wheeling patients down to basements in a state of panic, or fumbling for torches in the darkness. No more ringing in my ears after deafening explosions, or peering at faces covered in white dust. I can now walk happily in a park on a sunny day, knowing for certain that such a simple pleasure will not be shattered by a bomb blast. I feel enormously lucky. I have survived, and I owe it to those who didn't make it to make my life count for something. I will never take anything for granted again.

Flo noted:

London is very shabby looking, but even children playing in the rubble of bombed out streets are happy and excited. The East End is a shadow of its former self. There is nothing left of some streets, and houses which are still standing look as though they should be condemned. For now we are jolly and wave our flags, but there is much work to be done.

Like Rose, Dr Arthur Walker of St Thomas' Hospital expressed joyous relief tinged with sorrow: 'A lot of my school friends were killed, very few survived the war. I attended a school reunion and there were a hundred names on the wall.'[4]

Grace spent VE Day with her parents, but expressed her relief in a letter to one of her brothers:

Now all you young men can come home at last! What a day that will be … when all my brothers can march proudly through our front door. There's places in the East End that look like bomb sites, father says 'don't worry me gal' we'll rebuild it. Our hospital has been bashed to bits – needs a good lick of paint and a scrub up, but at least none of us need to wheel our patients past the white rabbits anymore. All that din – me chips and peas (knees) used to turn to jelly, good job nobody guessed as much.

Whilst the war in Europe was over, the war in the Far East continued until the Allies dropped an atomic bomb on Hiroshima on 6 August, and on Nagasaki three days later. Admiral Lord Mountbatten accepted the unconditional surrender of the Japanese in South East Asia and Singapore on 29 August, and General MacArthur accepted the Japanese surrender in Tokyo Bay on 2 September.[5] Nurse Phyllis Thoms, interned by the Japanese, described the way in which she realised the Japanese had been defeated:

We had a roll call every day and we weren't allowed out of our buildings until we had given our roll call. So we waited and waited and nothing happened. Then in the middle of the morning apparently the interpreter came in and told the British administrator that we were no longer at war. We were now friends! And we were all issued with a roll of lavatory paper, which we called the 'victory roll' because we have been very short of that as you can imagine.[6]

Rather bizarrely, nurses interned in Japanese prisoner-of-war camps were also issued with red lipstick shortly before their release. Japanese officials thought this gesture would make the women appear as if they had been well cared for during their period of captivity. In fact, it had the reverse effect, since most of the nurses weighed little more than 6 stone and red lipstick merely highlighted their gaunt features. Once settled back in Britain, actual accounts of their treatment filtered out to the press. The *British Journal of Nursing* expressed horror at the appalling atrocities perpetrated by the Japanese:

All women who have had the privilege to wear the uniform of a trained nurse hail with sincere rejoicings that noble band whose release from the hands of a murderous crew of inhuman wretches comes after three and a half years of imprisonment, yet who face life with unbroken and unquenchable spirit. The revolting brutalities perpetrated on helpless white enemies, men and women alike, show so similar a pattern of sadistic bestiality that the system must have been originated by those who held power in Japan. We hear of thirty Australian nurses who were machine-gunned to their death while still in the water, wading ashore after their ship had been torpedoed. The revelations coming from day to day of callous torture, of electric current playing on wet, nude bodies, of strenuous continuous work on starvation diet among malaria infested country, will make everyone who refuses to face the issue, acknowledge that the Japanese race is sub-human; beyond the pale of civilisation. To the lasting honour of those few nurses who have survived among the sixty five who were evacuated from Singapore, February 1942, just before it fell, they retained their courage and integrity, their desire to help those worse off than themselves, their sense of decency and humour during unspeakable mental and physical privations. The epic story may be related as a whole, meantime one must be satisfied to receive it piecemeal. Never has the uniform of a member of the nursing service earned such well deserved credit as it has in the innumerable instances in the tragic tumult of 1939–1945.[7]

With the cessation of hostilities, civilian and military medical organisations focussed on re-establishing normal services and rehabilitating war victims. Nurses were as instrumental in this process as they had been in support of the war effort. Nothing could have prepared military nurses, however, for the dreadful sights that lay ahead. The brutal horrors of Japanese prisoner-of-war camps could only be surpassed by the terrible inhumanity of German concentration camps, as a sickened BBC reporter described to his radio listeners:

Here over an acre of ground, lay dead and dying people. You could not see which was which except, perhaps, by a convulsive movement or the last quiver of a sigh from a living skeleton too weak to move. The living lay with their heads against corpses. Around them moved the awful, ghostly procession of emaciated, aimless people with nothing to do and no hope of life, unable to move out of your way and unable to look at the sights around them. This day at Belsen was the most horrible of my life.[8]

Nurse Anita Kelly recalled:

We emptied the hospital one evening and, when I came back the next morning the ward was full of men from Belsen. There they were with the shaved heads and it was my first experience of the number tattooed on their arm. Very few of them had anywhere to go. They had all lost their relatives or whole families in some cases. It was just kindness and patience they needed, tender loving care as it came to be called. But I don't think we had much effect on them. We treated them at the moment for whatever we could. We really couldn't at that time think how these people could possibly pick up the threads of life.[9]

Belsen was only one of many concentration camps established by the Germans for the systematic extermination of Jews. As the Allies approached the camps, however, camp commandants were forced to flee or risk being executed for war crimes. Thousands of prisoners being held in concentration camps were riddled with polio, diphtheria and typhus:

The German commandant of Belsen felt with the oncoming British forces the first thing that would happen would be this great rush of people. He had 60,000 men, women and children prisoners and, of them, about 15,000 were suffering from Typhus. If they had escaped into the countryside the disease would have spread. He was concerned about Germany but he knew just as well that the allies didn't want that sort of thing either. So he contacted Allied Headquarters and arranged that the British would move in ahead of time and a temporary truce would be declared to allow the British to take over the administration, even though the surrounding countryside was still in German hands. When we got there we were waiting. There was this German hospital and the mess. We thought we would have to work there and we went inside, but the Germans had moved so quickly. There were patients still on the operating table, and bodies in the mortuary. In the officers' mess there were lunch things on the table and food on the plates. They had just walked out![10]

In an attempt to combat disease and administer humanitarian aid, an alliance was formed between the International Red Cross and Red Crescent Societies of the Soviet Union. The World Health Organisation and similar bodies also made every effort to resettle all refugees and war victims. Amongst the nurses working with the United Nations Relief and Rehabilitation Administration to achieve this goal was Monica Baly, whose experience of war had given her a new outlook on the nursing and medical profession:

I resolved that once I was demobbed I would retrain as a health visitor. I wasn't going back to hospital. I realised that so much ill health was preventable. But the war made me. It taught me what I could do. It gave me courage in fact to do the things I could do. You just had to get on and do things, and it's by getting on and doing things that you find out what you can do.[11]

Other demobbed military nurses attempted to return to hospital life, but found civilian nursing rather mundane. Nurse Kitchener, writing in the *London Nurses' League Review*, expressed her feelings:

I have been very busy settling into civilian life after six years in the army. I returned to my old post as ward sister and find the children a great change after the men. I miss the moves of the army as I travelled quite a long way, Norway, M.E.F., Palestine and Egypt, France and Belgium. I was extremely pleased to see so much of Palestine especially Jerusalem and was lucky enough to meet my brother who was over with the Australian army. I had not seen him for fifteen years so we had a grand meeting. I went over to France five weeks after D-Day,

and wallowed in mud and rain (we were in a tented hospital) for weeks
before we moved to Belgium – a most interesting two day journey in
a lorry. My posting to Germany came at the same time as my release.
I was awfully sorry not to go.[12]

Newly demobbed nurses also discovered that their civilian counterparts
were completely out of touch with modern medical developments
and nursing techniques. New innovations in drug therapy, such as
penicillin, had not yet reached civilian hospitals, and techniques with
regard to blood transfusions, burns, wound treatments and chest
injuries had moved forward rapidly within the military nursing sector.
Military nurses, for instance, knew that early ambulation of post-
operative patients was not only possible but desirable, since early
ambulation prevented many post-operative complications. There were
ludicrous scenes on civilian wards, therefore, whereby demobbed
nurses were getting patients out of bed soon after surgery, only to find
that the very same patients were being hurried back into their beds
by long-established civilian nurses, the latter being convinced that
patients would die as a result of being moved out of their beds so soon
after their operations. Despite their best efforts to inform nurses in
the civilian sector of the positive medical changes developed within
the armed forces, civilian nurses clung rigidly to their old habits.
Even when penicillin was made available to hospitals, civilian nurses
continued to make totally unnecessary wound poultices. Thus the tug
of war on the wards continued unabated.

Members of the civilian nursing sector had also failed to get to grips
with military nurse officer status, believing that identification with the
'officer class' merely confirmed their membership of an elite social
class, and endorsed their authority over less-qualified nurses. The Royal
College of Nursing had established a Reconstruction Committee
chaired by Lord Horder, who produced reports in 1942, 1943 and
1949. Horder stressed that officer-class nurses were essential in order
to stimulate professional development. According to Horder, the main
function of officer-class nurses (who he recognised as being registered

nurses) was to provide professional leadership. But it was precisely this aspect of officer status that the majority of civilian nurses failed to grasp, and it was this failure that highlighted the civilian distortion of the modern military nursing framework.

Somewhat ironically, the Royal College of Nursing advisory pamphlet for demobbed nurses suggested that it was military nurses who were possibly out of touch with new nursing developments:

> When you come out of the forces you will have eight weeks in which to look around and take stock of your position. After the first wonderful weeks of reunion and rest, you will want to think about your plans for the future. You have seen much, and you will want to bring to civilian life a broadened outlook. It may be that during your period of service you concentrated on one special branch of nursing work, while possibly losing touch with developments in other fields.[13]

Although civilian nurses failed to comprehend the realities of the military officer role, they continued to be obsessed with the symbolic aspects of military protocol. But as Monica Baly subsequently observed, the failure to reform nurse education in the immediate post-war era resulted in nurses feeling 'out of their depth' in relation to medical innovations: 'The process of democracy in nursing was delayed because technical knowledge advanced with such rapidity that each generation was stranded on the beach of insecurity.'[14]

Nursing policies continued to be driven by status concerns and economic considerations. Even senior members of the World Health Organisation commented that, although British nurses were amongst the best practical nurses in the world, they were very poorly educated. They also stated that plans for the British National Health Service relied too heavily on the hospital to maintain civilian health – a problem, they concluded, which originated with doctors rather than nurses, since doctors relied on curative rather than preventative treatments to establish their individual reputations, and used their prestige to persuade government ministers to concentrate funds within the hospital environment.

As the International Council of Nurses acknowledged, by rejecting educational reform, nurses had effectively closed the door on professional development:

> It was felt by many people that the present system of nursing education was not always of the type that produced leaders of the ward unit or of the profession as a whole. In this last especially, there lies a danger that the profession may not always be organised for the greater participation in and contribution to the health service of the people.[15]

Failure to establish a nursing voice and take control of professional direction in the early stages of NHS planning had serious consequences. Nursing concerns were swallowed up amongst other healthcare professionals, and they were unable to influence policy for over a decade.

Furthermore, for all its celebrations of victory, Britain continued to experience wartime austerity. Rationing remained a feature of everyday life, and food shortages resulted in endless high street queues. The following poem written about a high street grocer and his shop in the run-up to Christmas 1945 amusingly captures the spirit of the time:

> Let us sing of the glories of Christmas in the days we remember afar,
> Ere peace and goodwill had been banished by the shadowy spectre of war.
> When Sid was a real Father Christmas, in his brightly lit Eign Street bazaar,
> Surrounded by satisfied housewives, who had come in from near and far.
> When his ticker beat time out correctly, and his critics said, 'he's got a nerve!'
> And the graph of his sales went a-souring in a beautiful positive curve.
> When his food store was crowded with turkeys, ducks, geese, tender

chickens and ham, and nuts, figs and dates, with bananas. And melons and strawberry jam.

Ah! Those were the days for the housewife, when shopping was easy and free, when a pound note was worth twenty shillings and she could by lashings of tea.

When points and the coupons we treasure were horrors that we never knew. When we saw what we wanted and got it without having to stand in a queue.

But now, though we get higher wages, our income we watch with concern, as it quickly gets smaller and smaller since all of us pay as we earn.

The children can't hang up their stockings, for the shops are depleted of toys, the girls have no tea sets nor dollies no Meccano and trains for the boys.

And Dad cannot get any whisky to drink to a Happy New Year.

His cigars are still out in Havana and there's hardly a hop in the beer.

Yet let us take heart and be merry, for although we are still in a mess.

We at least shall celebrate Christmas far better that Goering or Hess.

And if poultry is out of the question Mr Partridge still has plenty of fish.

To fill up 'the great open spaces' on our Christmas austerity dish.[16]

Notes

1   *Daily Mirror*, 3 February 1945.
2   Clark-Kennedy, A.E., *London Pride* (1979), p. 234.
3   *Daily Mirror*, 19 April 1945.
4   Walker, A., Oral history interview, Imperial War Museum Sound Archive ref: 17977/2/1-2.
5   For a detailed account of nursing in the Far East during the Second World War, please see: Starns, P., *Surviving Tenko: The True Story of Dame Margot Turner* (2010).
6   BBC Radio 4, *Frontline Females*, vol. 2.
7   *Journal of British Nursing*, December 1945.
8   BBC Radio 4, *Frontline Females*, vol. 2.
9   *Ibid.*

10 *Ibid.*
11 *Ibid.*
12 *Royal London Hospital Nurses' League Review*, no. xv, December 1946.
13 Royal College of Nursing Archive Edinburgh, ref R.C.N.17/8/1, pamphlet entitled 'The Re-settlement of Nurses', December 1945.
14 Baly, M., *Nursing and Social Change* (1980), p. 230.
15 Report of the International Council of Nurses 1947, quoted in the hospital minutes of Great Ormond Street Hospital, 16 September 1947.
16 Herefordshire County Record Office, K/38F/S4 *Hereford Times*, 15 December 1945.

15

POST-WAR
RECONSTRUCTION

During the 1945 general election, the British public removed Churchill from power and installed a new Labour Government, which was committed to introducing a National Health Service (NHS) and a comprehensive welfare state. However, contrary to popular belief, doctors and nurses were not particularly supportive of this policy. Most nurses were traditionalists and favoured the continuation of the voluntary hospital system, whereas doctors were concerned about their prestige and salaries, particularly the money they gained from private patients. Consequently, they fiercely resisted all initial attempts to bring them into a state-run health service. Indeed, Aneurin Bevan, the Minister of Health charged with establishing the NHS, was forced to make several concessions to increasingly truculent doctors. Public concerns were more transparent, with many reports and newspapers highlighting the professional stagnation of the medical profession:

The British Medical Association should occupy its energies not in political fighting, but in seeing that doctors under their control keep up with the job. The average general practitioner stands in knowledge today pretty well where he was when he attained his degree. It should be compulsory for doctors to attend hospitals for refresher training every five years. The blunders in diagnosis and surgical operations we ourselves know, are appalling. A surgeon in a case we are familiar with recently used a tube in a certain operation. The comment of a famous surgeon, who had to redo the operation months later was: 'A tube? Tubes have not been used in this operation since my student days,' and those days were nearly thirty years gone! If the health service depends for its working on the average general practitioner. With no further safeguards than now; then heaven help us. Progress British Medical Association, is what we want, not politics.[1]

Newspapers also drew parallels between the position of doctors and industrial disputes:

When dockers and other workers have gone on strike, it has been said of them that they were holding the country to ransom. I should say that this is precisely what the British Medical Association is doing. It seems that their interests are much more important that the welfare of the ordinary man in the street. Our proverb of the day is: The patient is not likely to recover who makes the doctor his heir.[2]

Certainly, general practitioners were set in their ways and had no opportunity to gain up-to-date knowledge, but even well-established surgeons tried to turn the clock back and return to the pre-war status quo. For instance, surgeons at The London Hospital demanded that theatres should once again be run by men rather than women. Yet, when Matron Alexander appointed two men to do precisely this task immediately after the war, they abandoned their posts after only six months, claiming they found the work far too strenuous. Not surprisingly, Matron Alexander announced this fact to the surgeons with considerable satisfaction, and the women were reinstated!

Rose and Gladys both celebrated this triumph with tea and fruit cake. Rose described their glee: 'We've been in fits of giggles all day about the men who can no longer run our theatres. Apparently it has all been far too much for them – the poor dear souls. What a load of codswallop!'

Diaries of nurses did not reveal their thoughts about the forthcoming NHS, but there were several complaints about continued rationing and austerity. Nurses were also extremely irritated when the new chancellor suggested that nurses needed to work harder to make up for shortages. He then proposed that nurses should no longer be considered a priority for extra rations because of the strenuous nature of their work. Outraged, the nursing press published a full-page, deeply sarcastic article about the subject:

A cut in our meagre rations is threatened. Nurses have no priority and thus they will have to carry out their arduous tasks on a less intake of energy and body building materials. This hardship will not affect older nurses as seriously as it will affect the younger ones. Now Mr Dalton's blessing, benevolent as it is, and most unexpected and staggering, will not supply the necessary calories required by nurses to carry out their daily tasks. Can he supply them with anything likely to appease hunger pangs more efficaciously than by his non-Episcopalian blessing?

Clothing coupons are to be in short supply over a longer period. Perhaps that won't affect nurses quite so badly, because they wear uniform for a long period of their earthly lives, which is coupon free. Still, their stockings wear out so quickly and their shoes get holes in them with such startling rapidity that one wonders if it might not be a good idea to copy the mediaeval Franciscans or Discalced Monks, and go barefooted or else press for exciting sandals made of nice soft leather, which leave bare toes and heels comfortably free!

'Ah' thinks one bright young thing. 'I will go abroad for holidays and stock up my wardrobe and have a jolly good feed and then return home ready for anything!' Unfortunately for her Mr Hugh Dalton thought first, and this time – without his blessing – he arranged that only a small amount of petty cash should accompany hungry British travellers abroad looking for 'extras.' So the bright young thing must think again. Once again our wily chancellor has the answer to it.

Nurses like everyone else must WORK! Yes – really work! Up to now nurses haven't worked at all, they've only THOUGHT they did. So now, what about taking a plot of ground in one's off-duty time and growing one's own tomatoes, spinach, asparagus, grapes and other luxuries, one has grown accustomed to having lately. On one's day off, why not 'volunteer' to work in a mill or factory, or even down a coal mine? Perhaps nurses sleep too long? Very well, cut down on sleep and volunteer for part-time night work in the nearest cottage hospital or relieve the hard pressed char woman and clean the corridors and front steps. There is always MORE WORK to be done if one looks hard enough for it.

You'll probably earn more money by undertaking these little extra jobs – perhaps you won't be quite sure what to do with it. Leave it to Mr Dalton – God bless him – he'll tell you what to do! After deducting his share of income tax, you may then buy War Savings or National Savings Certificates! Then, when you get older and the zest for living is departing and you no longer crave silk undies, nylons, creams and chocolates and glamorous holidays you will have plenty of money to buy all you require for your old age. Now isn't Mr Dalton a pet to think all this out for us?

So now we realise that for the great boon of being born and bred British, we must pay for the privilege. We've won the war, we've weathered the bombs and blast and now we've to crack and crush the crisis. Is this too much for British nurses to bear? No – no – a thousand times no – but let it be the last crisis, please! Some day – in the not too distant future – give us our perfumes and fine soaps, our stockings and shoes, our bright lights at night. Give us more nurses to share our burdens, and send us good cooks and chars without pains, and then, Mr Dalton, our work will be a pleasure and you won't have to plead with us to work or want. We'll work.[3]

There was no doubt, however, that severe labour shortages threatened to undermine government welfare policies and plans for post-war reconstruction. Indeed, as soon as the National Health Service was introduced, 30,000 hospital beds were closed because of a lack of nurses. The House of Lords spent a considerable time debating this crisis before suggesting that nurses would have to be obtained from the Colonies, and matrons would have to consider the prospect of encouraging male nurses into general nursing.

Lord Shepherd pointed out that:

More hospital beds are now occupied than before the war and many thousands are awaiting admission. There has been an increase of over 170,000 births per annum since 1940, which means that many more midwives are needed. The demand for nurses for other fields – for example industrial nursing and school nursing has greatly increased.[4]

Lord Crook, meanwhile, balked at the idea of introducing more men into the profession:

I stand here in the very difficult role of advocating the employment of male nurses while being quite certain that I like having had my brow smoothed by a ministering angel of the female sex. So we share that view of nursing. I regret that the economic situation and the manpower situation of the country forces me to suggest such outrageous things as taking away ministering angels and substituting male nurses.[5]

Others shared his reluctance:

Men nurses for mental cases and for other specialized forms of attention of course are quite right; but I do not know about general nursing. Perhaps it is only the sentimental attitude of a man who, fortunately, in his own case is hardly ever ill, but I am inclined to think that I would get better more quickly if I too had a ministering angel of the female sex. I question whether even the best trained man would do quite so well for me.[6]

Traditional prejudices towards male nurses were difficult to overcome. Yet, recently demobbed nurses who had worked alongside male RAMC orderlies were perfectly amenable to accepting male nurses within the field of general nursing practice. Opposition to men came not from ward level, but from those women working in the higher echelons of nursing society. Consequently, the RCN did not admit men into its ranks until 1960, and major teaching hospitals did not accept them for general nurse training until 1966. Matrons, in the meantime, had little option but to recruit large numbers of immigrant nurses, as Monica Baly noted:

> By the late 1940s, sixteen British colonies had established selection and recruitment procedures to ensure a steady intake of colonial recruits for the NHS. Enterprising matrons set off to the Caribbean, West Africa and the Philippines to recruit labour. In some cases they were so successful that you could find hospitals where almost all the staff below the rank of sister were of ethnic minority.[7]

Since most immigrants were channelled into assistant enrolled nurse training, immigration was not only used to alleviate nursing shortages, it was also used by the nursing profession to reinforce class distinctions, thereby elevating the position of registered nurses. As Trevor Clay, the first male president of the RCN, acknowledged:

> Enrolled nurse training represented one of the health services' biggest confidence tricks. Pupil nurse courses were filled in the 1950s and 1960s by recruits from Mauritius, the Philippines and elsewhere, who were misled into believing they were doing a registered nurse training that would put them on a secure career path. Too late, they discovered that the enrolled nurse qualification was the road to nowhere in the U.K. and virtually useless back home.[8]

Some hospitals were so obsessed with protecting status that they refused to contemplate running enrolled nurse courses. A senior nurse commented:

They thought they would lose status – the question of status came into it – to a certain extent they just wanted to train state registered nurses because it was a higher qualification, and I think they were frightened of the type of girl who would be coming in for state enrolled training.[9]

Since there were no promotional prospects associated with the assistant nurse grade, registered nurses were able to keep the grade suppressed just as they had done in the war. Cadet schemes were also misused. As Monica Baly recalled: 'Most schemes were just exploiting children.'[10]

Nursing within the NHS was not ideal, and was governed for the most part by senior members of the medical profession. Strong nurse leaders did exist in the civilian field, but they were based in Whitehall and were cut off from the rank and file of the profession. Most nurses followed the leadership of their hospital matrons, rather than nurses in Whitehall, so there was an unbridgeable gap in the formation of civilian nursing policy. Furthermore, the profession's overriding concern with nurse status seemed to overshadow all other issues, including those that affected patients.

There was no such gap within the military nursing sector. The chain of command between the matron-in-chief and her subordinates was always intact and, because military nurses had successfully resolved their status issues and had taken on board the correct interpretations of the officer role, nursing policy was more geared up to the needs of patients. The matron-in-chief paid as much attention to views that emanated from below as she did to views imposed from above. It should be acknowledged, however, that women in the armed forces competed at this time on the same terms as some men – in that they were single and without children. Moreover, in terms of professional expectations, the experiences of military and civilian nurses were worlds apart by 1950. Military nurses had become accustomed to a great deal of professional autonomy. They were able to prescribe certain drugs such as morphine, and give intravenous injections; simultaneously, their civilian counterparts were fighting to be allowed to take a patient's blood pressure.

Nevertheless, as the militarising Matron-in-Chief Dame Katherine Jones explained: 'Status cannot be created or justified by military scaffolding alone.'[11] Therefore, the military nursing corps embraced education and professional development with open arms. Consequently, senior officers from the various nursing corps were amongst the leaders in creating what has become institutionalised as the Brussels-based Senior Women's Officer Committee within NATO. At the time of its formation in the early 1970s, nursing officers were amongst the highest-ranking women throughout the North American and Western European forces.[12] In contrast, professional nursing in the civilian field suffered from severe stagnation: 'The civilian nursing hierarchy even as late as the 1970s relied upon a system of ranks and job specification rather than on an educational knowledge base supported by research into the value of nursing practice.'[13]

Military nurses also fared better than their civilian counterparts on the financial front. At the end of the war, the salaries of military nurses were initially aligned with civilian Rushcliffe pay scales, but these were deemed inappropriate for military officers and were rejected. Instead, military nurses successfully lobbied the Ministry of Defence to affirm their position vis-à-vis the Women's Royal Army Corps (WRAC), formerly the ATS, and to adjust their pay scales accordingly. A memorandum from the Secretary of State for War explained their position:

> The Q.A.R.A.N.C. will have powers of command over all women at all times and all men placed under their command. They will be subject to the Army Act as will the W.R.A.C. They do not understand why they should be the only class of officer, male or female, whose emoluments and conditions of service are directly based on civilians. They cannot be expected to be satisfied with different and inferior conditions of service, such as lack of time promotion, from those of W.R.A.C. officers with whom they will serve side by side.[14]

Ministry of Health officials were persuaded that military nurses needed to have higher salaries because of their role as officers of the armed forces. But they delayed making the salary scales for military nurses known for some time, because they feared that nurses entering the NHS would demand salary increases. They also feared that pay differentials would have an adverse effect on nurse recruitment.

Besides which, military nurses were still not satisfied. They argued convincingly that, because they were more qualified than WRAC officers when they entered military service, they should receive adequate recompense for these qualifications. After lengthy negotiations, the Ministry of Defence agreed to award the nurses a 'professional lead' in salary terms over other military women. Thus, in the immediate post-war era, military nurses had asserted their position as officers, and claimed a salary lead over both the civilian nursing services and fellow military women. Arrangements were also made with the GNC that would enable military matrons to recruit and train women for registration within the armed forces, rather than relying on the recruitment of nurses who had been trained in civilian hospitals. Thus, the status of military nurses continued to outstrip civilian nurses, and this was reflected in the number of applications to join the armed forces.

But it was not all doom and gloom in the civilian sector, and individual hospital matrons did initiate educational reform and structural change. Matron Clare Alexander, for instance, dropped the unique 'London Hospital' examination and introduced a weekly study day for her student nurses. Study days were usually followed by a day off-duty. She also changed the nature of nurse contracts. Prior to her matronship, nurses who had trained at the London for their registration for three years were expected to stay and work another full year as a staff nurse. Matron Alexander rightly perceived this restrictive contract to be a deterrent to recruitment, so she ended the fourth compulsory year. In order to retain her experienced senior nurses, she introduced a reward system whereby all nurses who had served the hospital for ten years were given three months' paid leave. In an attempt to broaden the outlook of the hospital, Matron Alexander negotiated with the House Committee to appoint at least 10 per cent of nurses from other hospitals. She succeeded in relaxing nurse discipline and significantly raised the reputation of The

London and its nurses. Many of her ideas for reform were copied by others. In 1951, she resigned her position in order to marry Sir John Mann, who was chairman of the hospital governors and associated with brewers Mann, Crossman and Paulin Ltd.

Matron Gladys Hillyers had also initiated educational reform, and justifiably gained the respect of all who worked with her at St Thomas'. However, a few weeks before the NHS was introduced, Matron Hillyers died of heart failure. Many of her nurses claimed that her demise was the result of heavy workload she had carried throughout the war. The *British Journal of Nursing* paid tribute in the 'passing of the bell':

> In the sudden passing of Miss Gladys Verena Hillyers, O.B.E. D.N. on Wednesday, May 19th, the nursing profession sustained a sad shock. At the time of her death she was President of the Royal College of Nursing, and during her distinguished career had held the post of Matron at St Thomas' hospital and Superintendent of the Nightingale training school from 1938–1946. After her retirement from that office Miss Hillyers continued her active interest in the various nurses' organizations, and her pleasant, happy personality inspired a ready response and affection from those with whom she came in contact, she will be greatly missed.[15]

Dame Kathleen Raven, whose diminutive frame and strong character earned her the nickname 'pocket battleship' whilst a sister at St Bartholomew's Hospital (Barts), became assistant matron at Barts, then matron at Leeds General Infirmary. Following some extensive tours of hospitals in North America, Matron Raven introduced 'beau parlours' – small rooms in nurses' homes where nurses could entertain their male guests. She became a member of the GNC and a Fellow of the Royal College of Nursing. More importantly, Dame Kathleen Raven became Chief Nursing Officer at the Department of Health in the 1960s. During this time, she asserted the rights of matrons to attend meetings of their respective hospital management committees, and advocated that nursing should always be focussed on the well-being of patients. Based on evidence gained during her visits to America and Canada, which demonstrated the value of intensive care nursing for critically ill patients, she persuaded the government to establish intensive care units in every hospital. Whilst she was working as Chief Nursing Officer, Dame Kathleen married Professor John Thornton Ingram, and she continued to play an active role in nursing issues until her death in 1999.

Whilst London matrons took a lead in nurse education and training programmes, in terms of nursing research, it was Lisbeth Hockey (Lisbeth Hochsinger), the bane of many a ward sister during her time at The London, who became a leading light in this area. This dynamic medical refugee from Nazi Germany became the Director of Nursing Research at Edinburgh University – the first nursing research unit in Britain. She died in 2004.

Monica Baly, as RCN representative for south-west England, spent much of her time striving to improve hospital and community conditions for nurses and patients alike. In later years, she became a tutor on the nursing degree course and wrote the basic set text for the curriculum. In her retirement, Monica studied to gain a degree in history and then her PhD. She became instrumental in setting up the RCN History of Nursing Society, wrote several books and articles, and lectured in nursing history. She was still writing up to her death in 1998.

As for Rose and her group of supportive friends, only self-doubting Gladys continued her nursing career. Rose married Harold in 1947. On her wedding day, she wore a silver-grey costume embellished with pale blue piping around the collar and sleeves. Flo, as promised, had sewn much of the outfit. Clothing coupons were still rationed and Flo had adjusted an existing costume. She had also embroidered small cornflowers on one of the lapels. All of Rose's family and friends attended the ceremony, and the whole of the Barking Road came out to wish her well. Rose and Harold eventually had seven children. Harold left the army and became an ambulance driver. They remained in the East End. Flo abandoned nursing in favour of becoming a seamstress, and she married a teacher in 1950. Grace continued to be active within the Girl Guide movement but gave up nursing when she married the owner of a traditional pie and mash cafe in 1951. Given her love of food, all her friends agreed that it was the best possible match! Gladys eventually married a doctor, but was unable to have children. This predicament may have influenced her decision to remain within the nursing profession. She did, however, fulfil her desire to travel, as she and her husband moved to Australia in the 1960s.

Doctor Arthur Walker, who sustained a devastating head injury at St Thomas' during one of the early air raids, had managed to resume his medical training in the spring of 1941. He left England in 1948 to establish a medical school in Nigeria. He had a very interesting career and became a lecturer in medicine. Following his retirement, he and his wife lived in Dorset. His daughter followed his family tradition and became a doctor at St Thomas'. Doctor Archibald Clark-Kennedy, who worked unceasingly through the Blitz, remained at The London. Writing about that difficult time, he praised his colleagues:

On the House Governor, Henry Brierley, the entire responsibility for the safety of the hospital had rested and as lay sector officer it had been his duty to cope with every other hospital emergency nearby. Never did he falter, either. He inspired confidence everywhere and his capacity for quick and right decisions had proved invaluable again and again. To the friendly disposition of the surveyor must be attributed the efficiency of his staff. George Neligan's experience as a surgeon in the First World War stood him in good stead but his personality had contributed something to the psychology of the situation which was even more valuable. The life, it is true, suited his unhurried Irish temperament. There he would sit hour after hour, his cup of coffee or tankard of beer before him, smoking cigarette after cigarette, his meditations only interrupted by fits of coughing, an unparalleled example of imperturbability to all who were privileged to work with him. Conscious of everything that was going on, he was always there when wanted; watching quietly to see that everything was done right, never saying a word unless something would be done wrong if he didn't intervene. Even then, never did he claim credit for a right decision. Never have I come across another man who managed to go through the motions of doing so little and yet at the same time succeeded in doing so much.[16]

George Neligan, meanwhile, paid his own tribute to those who had worked with him:

It is impossible to find words to express one's appreciation of the behaviour of the whole staff whether they were sisters, nurses, medical or lay. They were a grand team who never faltered. Going round the wards during a raid it was good to see the sisters and nurses working all out, the only noticeable difference from peace-time being their tin hats, often worn at jaunty angles on their heads, in spite of the noise of the guns and falling bombs repeatedly shaking the building. Another section of the staff I shall never forget, were the old night scrubbers. Many of these were over seventy, and for untold years they had turned up at 6am to clean the same area of the hospital floor. Now, no matter how severe the blitz, or whether transport had been knocked out and they had to walk from their homes, many of which had been ruined by bombs, these old ladies turned up to time, and pail in hand would settle down to their long-accustomed task, only stopping to argue from time to time with their scrubber friends as to who had had the biggest bomb dropped near her in the raid.[17]

During the immediate post-war years, senior nurses and medical staff featured prominently in the New Year's Honours List. Many of them also received medals for their heroic achievements. Over 3,000 military nurses had died as a result of wartime service (this compares with just over 300 for the ATS), and many more suffered psychological and physical scars as a result of the conflict. There were no comparable figures for civilian nurses, only a general recognition that along with other hospital staff, ambulance drivers and ARP workers, they ran the greatest risk of being killed or severely injured during the Blitz. Across Britain, approximately 87,000 civilians were injured, and over 43,000 were killed between

September 1940 and the end of May 1941. Over 20,000 of these were killed in London, 3,000 in one night alone. It was with a great deal of pride, therefore, and a sense of triumph, that the government Home Intelligence Service reported that the morale of Londoners and their children throughout the war was beyond praise. In the grim, terrifying months of the Blitz, courageous nurses had simply got on with their work. During the months when Britain stood alone against a seemingly invincible enemy, in defiance of nurses' home rules, Nurse Gladys Tyler had pinned a quote from Elizabeth Barrett Browning to her bedroom door: 'Happy are all free peoples too strong to be dispossessed. But blessed are those among nations who dare to be strong for the rest.' It is highly likely that all London nurses endorsed these sentiments, and could justifiably claim, as Rose did, when writing her final wartime diary entry: 'Every single one of us has played a part in saving London.'

Notes

1   *Daily Mirror*, 27 April 1945.
2   *Ibid.*
3   *British Journal of Nursing*, September 1945.
4   Hansard House of Lords Official Reports, vol. 159, 9 November 1948.
5   *Ibid.*
6   *Ibid.*
7   Baly, M., 'Leadership and the Legacy of War', unpublished conference paper given at the RCN's Legacy of War Conference 1995, p. 5.
8   Clay, T., *Nurses, Power and Politics* (1987), p. 105.
9   Oral History Transcript N19, Wellcome Unit for the History of Medicine.
10 Baly, M., Oral history interview, 7 November 1995.
11 Jones, Dame Katherine, speaking at the Association of Matrons conference in 1944, National Archive ref: WO/222/178.
12 Enloe, C., *Does Khaki Become You?* (1983), p. 114.
13 Maclean, U., *Nursing in Contemporary Society* (1974), p. 108.
14 National Archive ref WO/32/12330.
15 *British Journal of Nursing*, June 1948, p. 67.
16 Clark-Kennedy, A.E., *London Pride* (1979), p. 222.
17 *Ibid.*, pp. 222–23.

SELECT BIBLIOGRAPHY

Baly, M., *Nursing and Social Change* (1980).

Baly, M., *Florence Nightingale and the Nursing Legacy* (1986).

Bowman, G., *The Lamp and the Book: Royal College of Nursing History* (1967).

Brown, M., *Put that Light Out: Britain's Civil Defence Services at War 1939–1945* (1999).

Cambray, P. & Briggs, G., *The Official History of the Humanitarian Services of the British Red Cross Society and the Order of St John of Jerusalem 1939–1947* (1947).

Clark-Kennedy, A.E., *London Pride: The Story of a Voluntary Hospital* (1979).

Clay, T., *Nurses, Power and Politics* (1987).

Curnock, G.C., *Hospitals Under Fire but the Lamp Still Burns* (1941).

Dickens, M., *One Pair of Feet* (1942).

Gardiner, J., *The Blitz: The British Under Attack* (2010).

Kynaston, D., *A World to Build* (2007).

Lowe, R., *The Welfare State in Britain Since 1945* (1993).

Maclean, U., *Nursing in Contemporary Society* (1974).

MacNalty, Sir A.S. (ed.), *History of Second World War: UK Medical Services*, 21 volumes (HMSO, 1952–72).

Overy, R., *Why the Allies Won* (1995).

Salvage, J., *The Politics of Nursing* (1985).

Splane, R. & Splane, V., *Chief Nursing Officer Positions at the Ministry of Health* (1995).

Titmuss, R., *Essays on the Welfare State* (1958).

White, R., *The Effects of the National Health Service on the Nursing Profession 1948–1961* (1985).

INDEX

By the same author

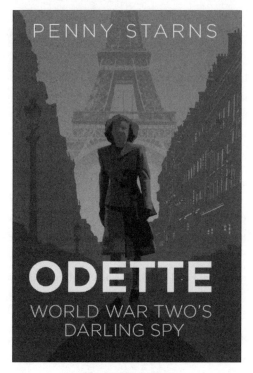

PENNY STARNS

ODETTE
WORLD WAR TWO'S
DARLING SPY

978 0 7509 8437 9

Penny Starns delves into SOE personnel files to reveal the true story of wartime heroine Odette Brailly and the officer who posed as her husband, revealing the truth of her mission and the heart-breaking identity of her real betrayer.

The History Press

The destination for history
www.thehistorypress.co.uk

By the same author

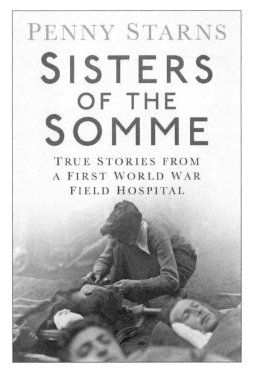

978 0 7509 6162 2

Based on the previously unpublished stories of nurses and medical staff, *Sisters of the Somme* is a heartwarming account of the joys and sorrows of life in an extraordinary Somme field hospital.

The History Press

The destination for history
www.thehistorypress.co.uk

By the same author

978 0 7524 6031 4

Penny Starns takes a new look at
the children whose parents refused
to bow to official pressure and kept
their beloved children with them
throughout the war. Because of their
unique position at the heart of the
action, these forgotten children offer
us a priceless insight into the true
grit and reality of the Blitz.

The destination for history
www.thehistorypress.co.uk